Popularity

Growing UP Girls Book 3

by

Suzanne Rudd

HHH Press

Suzanne Rudd

This is a work of fiction. Names, characters, places, and incidents are products of the author's imagination or are used fictitiously. Any resemblance to actual events or locales or persons, living or dead, is entirely coincidental.

Popularity Copyright © 2022 by Suzanne Rudd

All rights reserved. Except as permitted under U.S. Copyright Act of 1976, no part of this book may be reproduced, stored in a retrievable system, or transmitted by any means without written permission from the author.

ISBN: 9798848683875

Imprint: HHH Press

Why This Story?

Growing up, I was bullied for something that wasn't my fault. Book 1 in this series tells that story. It taught me to be tougher and more defensive. Decades later, I can tell you that's not always necessarily a good thing.

Bullying now has more attention than when I grew up, but it also has more avenues for destruction.

New technology and societal changes bring new ways to humiliate and bully anyone and more reasons people can think of to bully. That's not better.

Teens learn from their environment—their friends and family. And often that perpetuates hate from generation to generation. Peer pressure and personal desire can also generate hate.

Why do they do it? Why do they care who someone else is? Sometimes it's a lack of self-esteem, and often it's a projection of their own perceived shortcomings, but most of the time, it comes down to one thing... control.

But understanding and recognition empowers. In this Growing Up Series of books, I address growing trials and triumphs in all avenues through the eyes of the individual girls and how they handle it all and come out better on the other side.

Suzanne Rudd

Table of Contents

Content Notice: This book is designed for readers 12+ years old and over. There are situations surrounding cyberbullying and death in this text to illustrate perils of some teenage behavior, though these topics are handled delicately. The chapters are starred below. Those with sensitivities to these topics may want to consult an adult before reading.

Chapter One—Meet Mel	5
Chapter Two—The Glam Squad	13
Chapter Three—Open Door	20
Chapter Four—The Mascot	27
Chapter Five—Poms	36
Chapter Six—The Game	43
Chapter Seven—Homecoming Queen	52
Chapter Eight—Glam Mel	63
Chapter Nine—The Dance	81
Chapter Ten—High Maintenance	102
Chapter Eleven—Cyberbullying*	117
Chapter Twelve—New Life	133
Chapter Thirteen—The Accident*	145
Chapter Fourteen—The Aftermath*	155
Chapter Fifteen— New Day	171

Chapter One
Meet Mel

You know how some things go together and some don't? Spaghetti and meatballs, movies and popcorn and shoes and socks are famous pairs, but pickles and ice cream, popcorn and milk and spaghetti and tuna are definitely not.

I always felt I am one of the things that don't go with any other. I'm Melinda.

Melinda was my grandmother's name. She died before I was born, so my mother wanted me to have her name. My mom says grandma was a spitfire, but unfortunately all I inherited was her name.

I'm one of the unseen people; I exist in the shadows on the outside looking in. I pride myself on blending into my background, like camouflage. And it helps my art; it makes me an observer. I watch people and I draw what I see.

I notice the shy boy desperately trying to ask the girl he likes for a date, while the girl's fruitlessly trying to encourage him by flirting.

I spot the band, drama and choir students who can't help themselves from breaking into song at any given moment, everywhere they are. It must be nice to have that kind of talent.

I observe the awkward outsider kids at their lunch table, the ones who luckily found each other and are free to happily be themselves. They seem like birds flying in whatever direction the wind blows them.

And I spy some of the football team acting like the biggest men on our high school campus by torturing poor freshmen and mathletes, spilling their lunches and knocking their books down.

When I draw this type of bullying behavior, I usually illustrate them as funny-looking monsters with big snaggy teeth with hunched backs and horns all over their bodies. Sorry, not sorry—that's how I see them, so their outsides match their insides.

But I also view the cracks in their armor when some of them are alone and the power of numbers is gone. On their own, I note their confidence and self-esteem often fade as some struggle to keep up in class. Without numbers, they are only one.

When you take yourself out of the narrative and open your eyes, unrestrained by outside influence, you see things as no one else can.

My favorite subjects of observation are the beautiful girls in school. They call themselves "The Glam Squad."

Every day, I can't wait to see what they're wearing or how they do their hair. Drawing them is pure pleasure.

They seem to splash right out of the posts and videos of *Seventeen* magazine and *Teen Vogue*. Designer shoes, clothes, backpacks… the bling is literally blinding.

I'm the plainest Jane in the world. My curly, frizzy hair is an uncontrollable mess and my clothes are hand-me-downs, but secretly I have a passion for everything beautiful. I follow every fashion influencer on social media and never miss a thing.

I have to admit, I look at them with awe and envy. They're so confident and pretty that they pull the attention of everyone in their wake like magnets like goddesses. It's amazing.

So when I draw them, I show them on pedestals or in the clouds surrounded by stars and wind gliding like flowing doves as they wield their god-like influence over the students here.

They're truly unique rarities in the normal student body. Then again, aberrations describe everything I experience at this school.

Last year, the high school in my area closed and the district redrew the boundaries to split up the kids into neighboring schools.

The administration says it was a cost-cutting measure, but I heard many parents say it's an attempt to integrate kids from poorer and working-class families with rich kids. I understand there were even lawsuits to prevent it from happening, but it did anyway.

I heard one teacher call it "a sociological representation of the real world in a microcosmic bubble of high school." Makes me feel a little bit like a Petri dish in a vast trial of humanity, as seen through a teenage lens.

But as the authority figures experiment with their live subjects, one thing they always fail to factor in is reality. It's tough enough to be a teen with a constantly changing body and outsider perception of yourself. The constant struggle is just to exist every day and try to learn something. But add in the separation of culture and wealth and it can be a continental divide that's difficult for a young person to navigate.

To double the pain, all my friends since elementary school went to the other high school. So, I started as a freshman last year completely and utterly alone.

The first day of school was like waking up on another planet. From the fancy phones carried by all the students and designer wardrobes to the cars parked in the parking lot, it all smelled of money.

In my head-to-toe Goodwill hand-me-downs, I feel like Cinderella going to the ball in rags instead of a gorgeous gown. And there was no fairy godparent around. I definitely don't fit in.

Very quickly, I became fascinated by the extraordinary and flagrant display of wealth. It's so different from the life I lead, the only child of a single mother with two jobs living in a tiny rental home on the "other" side of town.

I think that's why I'm so captivated by the glamor girls in the squad. They're out of this world. It's something I can never hope for, but can enjoy from the outside looking in.

I watch and record this high school experiment in my drawings. I don't know what I'll do with them, if anything, but now in my second year, I have accumulated 15 sketchbooks so far. I fill about one a month. Along with pencils and gel and sparkle pens, I buy them on clearance or at garage sales—anywhere I can get them cheap. I babysit in my neighborhood and do odd jobs after school to make money for my art habit. I've also learned to use every square inch of paper and every bit of pencil lead down to the nub.

For months, I sat and drew without notice—until I met Ev. She's remarkable, the self-proclaimed queen of the school outcasts.

She's from the other side of the tracks, literally, in a section of town that has constant railroad traffic from freight and commuter trains. It's very noisy and sometimes even shakes like a mini-earthquake.

But Ev is a warrior. She takes no prisoners and gives no apologies for the way she lives her life. Her hair is usually spiky, but she changes the length, style and color as often as the richies change their expensive sneakers. And she always picks the most electric thing to wear. She's a rock musician, so I guess that's part of the uniform.

She's edgy and cool and calls me Mel. I like that. It makes me seem trendy, even though I'm not.

It's strange. I crave what makes others unique, but I don't want to stand out.

We first met when I was in my usual chameleon mode, trying to blend in and draw what's around me. Most of the time, this worked and people left me alone, but she noticed me and invited me to sit with her group.

I declined. I told her I like to maintain focus on my artwork. But really, I use that as a cover. I'd like to have friends, I think. I just don't know how to fit in.

For weeks, she invited me every day and asked to see my work. I was stunned. No one ever acknowledged me or my work.

To me, they're just doodles of what I see through my mind's eye. But with her creative palate, Ev sees them better than I do.

"These are wonderfully detailed representations of people and things showing their innermost feelings and true colors." She pointed to a few drawings and explained what she saw in them.

"This picture of a man reading a book shows the depth of his interest in the subject and the wonderment reflected in his face. And this drawing of an older dog with a ball in his mouth, but his eyes show the young pup who always wants to run and play. You see inside people—their emotions, wants and needs. It's a special gift."

That was it. We bonded over our creative spirits. I prefer a one-on-one friendship and she never pressures me to do otherwise.

She laughs when I draw her exploits. Whether she's standing up for bullied kids or trying to make changes in the school to benefit everyone, she's a superhero. And that's how I draw her, because that's what I see.

She always laughs at my depictions of her.

"Why do you always draw me with muscles and a big 'A' on my chest?" she asks.

"Because you are the strongest person I know and I think you're incredible," I answer.

I love her artistic soul and continually admire her bravery and talent, in spite of her obstacles.

It's not easy being openly gay in high school. There are only a few others who are out. She takes on everything and leads the charge for acceptance of every disadvantaged kid in the school, no matter what.

I may have only one friend, but I'm glad it's her.

Chapter Two
The Glam Squad

It's funny how they say one decision can change your life forever. It's true. It happened to me.

In my attempt to remain invisible, I travel through the halls with my head down to avoid making eye contact with people. I've become a pro at walking this way without any collisions. I guess I've developed a kind of radar. I know when people are coming.

But this time, when heading to my locker, I see an imaginative pair of purple Converses painted with an epic clash of rainbow-colored unicorns fighting fire-breathing dragons. The intriguing blend of colors draws my complete attention and before I know it, I'm on the ground with my sketchbooks open all over the floor. And above me is the human wall I hit.

"Keep your head up next time, honey," the sweet lilty Southern voice laughs.

When I look up, I see Alyssa. I recognize her tall stature beautiful long blond hair, blue eyes with sparkling golden eyeshadow and passion for white and gold attire. She's a member of The Glam Squad. In my drawings, she appears as Aphrodite, with her swaying frock of golden fabric and flowing hair, attracting everything and everyone in her path, especially boys.

"I'm sorry. I hope I didn't hurt you," I say as I stagger to my feet and frantically pick up the mess strewn all over the floor.

"These are spectacular!" Alyssa shouts and grabs one sketchbook opened to a drawing.

"Did you draw these?" she asks.

"Yes, they're just scribbles of things I see," I reply in a soft voice. I pick up the other books and put them in my backpack.

"Draw me," Alyssa says excitedly and thrusts her hand on her hip, striking a pose.

"Hmm, I don't sketch people posing like a model. I usually draw them while they're doing something and always when they don't know I'm watching. It's more natural that way," I say apologetically.

"All right then, eat with us at lunch and draw me while I'm not looking," she says and glides down the hallway, motioning me to follow her.

It's a strange sensation. One of the people I greatly admire from afar for over a year is talking to me. And she wants me to draw her. She likes my work.

I'm giddy, gleeful and dumbfounded, but I obediently follow.

Trailing behind her, I realize how she bounces a little when she walks, as if floating on air with her toes acting as takeoff points with the ground. I can't help but smile; I've never seen anyone move like that.

She leads me to the outside lunch area and directly to her table. I shudder when I see where we're going—to the popular table. There they all are. I can't believe I'm this close to them.

In my ecstatic fantasy view, I imagine the table perched on a glittery cloud with pastel-colored auras all around the girls and golden fairy dust rising in the air with an ethereal chorus of "ahs" singing as harps strum along. I know that's not reality, but after all, it is the cool lunch table.

In all the days I've watched them, secretly scribbling from the bleachers while they laugh and talk, I never thought I'd be invited to sit at their table.

The Glam Squad is a collection of the prettiest and most popular girls in school. I knew them all by name as if they were celebrities. They're the homecoming princesses, prom queens and most of the poms dance cheer squad. They have the school and the student body in the palms of their hands.

I stand there frozen, staring at them. Awestruck, I forget everything in my head until Alyssa breaks my trance.

"Sit across from me so you can draw my face. This is my best side," she says eagerly as she contorts herself into a fake model pose on the picnic table bench.

I place my sketchbook on the table and pull a variety of gel pens in various colors out of my bag. I normally sketch in pencil, but I want to impress them. I think they'll like the pretty colors and sparkles of the pens, which give my drawings a pop art kind of feel.

I take a long look at Alyssa and drink her in, as I do with all my subjects. I don't know if I'm nervous or if her pose is throwing me off, but I just can't get a read on her depth.

"I promise to get your best side, but you don't have to sit still like that. I do my best work when it's relaxed and spontaneous," I tell her.

She shrugs and begins gabbing with the other girls. They're all talking loudly at the same time. I'm not really sure who's saying what or how they're eating, as none of them seem to take a breath.

No one notices me. I'm like the table or the air—just there. But that's good for me. I need room to think and create without interruption.

I observe them intensely—every facial expression and every movement. Their hair flows back and forth as they move quickly talking with their hands while expertly drinking their diet soda and eating. It's electric.

All the sudden it hits me. I doodle with a speed and enthusiasm I never experienced before. Like a machine, I grab pen after pen in rapid succession, drawing not only Alyssa, but everything around her.

This is it. This is my chance to run with their crowd. I don't fit in now, but if they like what they see, maybe someday, I could.

Finally, I finish just before the bell and show them all. It's a colorful representation of them relaxing on a glittery blue cloud with golden dust rising up. They're all dressed in flowing colored fabrics with their hair gently surging in the wind, like goddesses. It's exactly what I see when I first approached their table.

I'm so nervous. Only Ev has seen my work before, no one else. I hold my breath, hoping and praying they like it.

"OMG that is stellar!" Alyssa shouts. "I love how we're in a heavenly pool or something, just waiting for Jesus."

"Alyssa, really? She's depicted us as Greek goddesses on Olympus," corrects Amanda in her authoritative tone.

Amanda's the leader of the squad. She's easily the most confident in the group and also the most striking, with her long jet-black hair in a sleek ponytail and catlike brown eyes accentuated with black eyeliner.

"Of course, I see it now," Alyssa says sheepishly and looks down.

Amanda puts out her hand and I give her the drawing on command.

"I like it. Alyssa can have this one. Tomorrow, come back and draw us another way," she says, placing the drawing down and walks away with her head held high as the others instinctually march behind her.

I'm over the moon. They like it and want me to come back. I have one foot in the door.

I hand the drawing to Alyssa, who immediately regains her peachy Southern outlook.

"You're very talented. Thank you." She takes the drawing and bounces after the others, leaving me alone again.

Ideas are percolating in my head. If I can draw them individually and as a group in interesting ways, maybe they'll let me stay. I'm so close.

Chapter Three
Open Door

For the first time in my life, I spend so much time dressing for school, I almost miss my bus. I want to look my best for the girls, so I pick my nicest outfit, a stone-washed jean jacket with a purple T-shirt and a blue pleated skirt with my white gym shoes. And I pull my hair into a side ponytail.

Every morning, class seems to go in slow motion as I intently watch the clock in anticipation of my lunch date with The Glam Squad. Finally, the buzzer for fifth hour rings in my head like the starting bell for the Kentucky Derby. I'm so excited, I swiftly move my way through the crowded hallways of passing students and head outside.

When I open the glass door and immediately see the glitter and glam of their outfits, I glance at my reflection. Even my best effort to glam up is still bad. My hair is curly, frizzy and unmanageable; my face looks pale; and my outfit is just... plain and boring.

I approach their table slowly and stealthily, afraid they may have forgotten about me. To remind them, I have my sketchbook out so they can see my doodles. All night I drew individual pictures of all of them as a start, so now I can continue during the lunch period when I have the models right in front of me.

Since Amanda is the leader of the group and the key to my success, I put her sketch on the outside and walk toward her.

"Amanda, I started this drawing of you last night. I thought I could finish it during lunch so I can get your face just right," I say, handing her the picture.

I bite my lip for what seems like forever, hoping she'll say yes.

"I like it. Ok, sit down," she says, handing me the picture while looking in the opposite direction.

I'm in!

Amanda, Alyssa, Brittany, Ashley and Chloe make up The Glam Squad. It's cute. Their names are just like the ABC's. I wonder if that happened organically.

As far as I can tell, inclusion in the group is at the discretion of the leader and you can be kicked out at any time for any action that they don't like. It isn't a democracy and there are no second chances.

Alyssa is the pretty blond, blue-eyed, tall and skinny model type in the group. She spends a lot of time perfecting her poses and makeup to accentuate her facial expressions, and her fashion instincts are impeccable. *Teen Vogue* shows fashions after Alyssa is already wearing them. But she favors dressing in gold and white. She wants to start a new trend.

Brittany is a petite girl with chestnut brown hair, brown eyes and a full figure. She's fresh-faced in her makeup and dresses in a lot of bright colors like light blues, yellows and lime greens and doesn't show her chest. She's like the girl next door.

Chloe's the smartest one in the group, as she maintains an "A" average, and is the only one with rich dark auburn hair and hazel eyes. Besides poms, she's a world-class gymnast and is nearly always seen in dance pants and matching jackets in silver metallic and black colors.

Ashley is the best dancer in the school. She's tall, like Alyssa with long blond hair and blue eyes. Like a cover girl, you never see her in anything that's not the newest and best style. Every look is unique, perfect and pink. It's her signature color.

Beyond their slight differences in appearance, there is little individuality in the group. All of them have long hair and wear complete makeup every day with eyeliner, lashes, lipstick and blush or bronzer. Their shiny nails are perfect every day with no messes or chipping.

I wonder how they get their nails so flawless. Every time I wash my hands, I get a little chipping in the color. I doubt that they never wash their hands, so there must be a way.

Their clothes vary in style, but there are common elements of glitter, bedazzling, and jewelry, all in the most cutting-edge styles. And they all wear some kind of wedge sneakers, sandals or glittery heels. No plain white sneakers or loafers; everything is regimented and strictly followed.

The girls quickly begin their daily routine of gossiping and reading aloud posts and videos from Instagram, Snapchat and TikTok on their phones while nibbling on their small salads and French fries and sipping diet sodas with straws. Alyssa says it's important to eat and drink without messing your lipstick, so small food and straws are essential.

It's difficult to understand them, as they all talk fast and speak over one another. But when I tune my ears to their frequency, it comes in clearer.

"Did you see the new outfit in *Teen Vogue* today? I think it's absolutely stellar," Alyssa says.

"*Seventeen* posted that days ago. Yesterday's news," Ashley chimes in.

"I like the floral spring jumper that new pop star is wearing on Instagram today," Ashley says.

"Really? I think it makes her look fat. You never add extra width," Alyssa counters.

"Ooh, here's a post about a certain color guard captain with her new mathlete boyfriend," Brittany laughs.

Alyssa looks over her shoulder at the picture. "He's kinda cute," she says.

The other girls stop talking and gaze at her in astonishment.

"He's a mathlete," Chloe says in shock.

"She can expect her stock to go way down in the ribbon-waving squad." Amanda lets out a single chuckle while looking in a mirror, touching up her lipstick.

I scribble on Amanda's picture as I observe them with immense interest. But I want to listen to. If I want to be one of them, I need to know their secrets. That'll have to be for another day; the goal now is to be accepted and included.

I scramble to finish my drawing before the bell sounds the end of lunch.

"All done. What do you guys think?" I smile proudly.

They all stare at it in astonishment and silently nod their approval, waiting for Amanda to speak.

"I like it. You captured the essence of my beauty. Thank you." She grins and takes the drawing.

In synchronicity, all the other girls grin in agreement, begging for me to draw them too.

"Tomorrow, you may come back to portray Alyssa. After all, she brought you to our attention. What's your name?" Amanda declares.

"Melinda," I say meekly.

She leaves the table and the others follow in a coordinated line behind her.

I'm can't believe it. She asked my name! That's something.

As I gather my gel pens and pencils and sketchbook together, Ev sees me and suddenly comes toward me with a look of shock and disbelief on her face.

"What are you doing at the twaddle table?" she asks firmly.

"I'm just doing some drawings for them. It's no big deal," I say flippantly so she doesn't suspect my glee.

"I couldn't believe my eyes when I saw you with them. Be careful—they're evil users. Just give them what they want and be done with them as quick as you can. I hope you're charging them a lot," she warns and walks with me back to class.

As I sit through sixth period history, I keep thinking about Ev. I don't want her to know that I long to be part of The Glam Squad. She hates them. She calls them the twaddle troupe because she says they follow each other around like baby ducks marching in a row behind their mother.

But even though she's my very best friend, she doesn't understand my problem. She knows who she is and she loves it. She has the confidence to be herself every minute of every day.

Other than my art, I have no idea who I am. I'm invisible. I just blend into the background of this school. If I miss school for days, only Ev would know or care.

Popularity

That's why I like the glam girls. People notice and envy them. If one of them isn't at school, every student would know it. There may even be a worldwide manhunt.

I hate lying to her, but she treats it like the Civil War we're learning about in history class—the blue and the gray. She draws the line in the sand and doesn't want anyone crossing it. To me, there are no lines, just sand.

Chapter Four
The Mascot

For a week, I go to The Glam Squad's table every day, sketching a different girl and giving her my illustration.

I watch them while I'm drawing and sometimes even sneak a question in here and there about clothes, makeup and hair. Since they're grateful for their pictures, they're sweet and generous enough to answer my questions and give me advice.

Brittany has curly hair too, but hers is stylish and orderly, while mine continually frizzes out like those Chia pets you used to see on TV.

"Gotta have my product. I use a calming cream and special shampoo to keep the curls shapely and so they lie nicely," she says.

She's right—her hair is precise, as though someone sculpted the curls in a clay statue of a goddess.

I try it and it works a little bit. I think it takes time, but soon I'm able to add bejeweled and color clips in my hair to make it look decent.

Brittany is also the makeup queen. She knows more about lashes, liner and lipstick than the people who sell them.

I ask her about makeup one day and she does my colors for me. According to her chart, my pale skin is perfect for a little pink blush and pink gloss with some glitter and shine. And she says to use a light brown liner.

Luckily, my mom has the same complexion as me and had a few things I can use. I'll save up my babysitting money to buy more.

Chloe lets me in on her nail secret—many clear topcoats. She applies multiple coats a day to keep the undamaged look and invented a way to wash her hands using cloths that don't allow water to touch her nails. She also goes to the salon twice a month.

That's a little beyond my means, so I try some peel on and off nail polish, topcoat and a manicure kit I found at the dollar store. I watch YouTube videos to learn how to do it all. I think my nails look good. The topcoats make the nails shine, but then I can't get the peel-off polish off easily. I have to use turpentine from my paints. It's still a work in progress.

Ashley is the one look to for clothes advice. She sews and designs her own clothing. She takes store-bought items and bedazzles and bejewels "Ashify" them to make her own creations. She could be the next big designer.

Following her example, I bedazzle my jean jacket with floral appliques I got at the dollar store, a glue gun and a jeweled pin my mom gave me and pair it with a cute pull-on skirt and floral top I found at Goodwill.

The glam girls compliment me on my outfit, which sends me soaring like a rocket in joy.

"You look nice today, Melanie," Amanda says.

I shot up in my seat with pride at her compliment. She didn't remember my name exactly, but it's close.

"Hmm. You don't look like a Melinda anymore. That's too old-fashioned for your new look," she says.

The girls banter a few nicknames about like Linda, short for Melinda, or Penny or Gelly, after my gel pens, but I don't want to change my name too much.

"Some of my friends call me Mel," I interject.

"Mel. I love it. That's cool," Amanda says.

I put on a simple smile, but on the inside, I'm jumping up and down. Amanda says my name is cool. Now I need to earn that name by keeping my fashion points up.

Trying to emulate their designs and style is hard to do on a budget. The trends at the Goodwill store are usually from long ago, that's why people discard them. Unless you have a good eye or can sew and change them, they're not cool.

But I'm still trying—and making leaps and bounds in my personal look. It's a lot of work and maintenance and does require more money. I ask my mom for some extra work at her main job. She does accounting for a food manufacturer and they have some part-time positions for a couple hours a day boxing up their products. It's not glamourous, but with that and a few dog-walking gigs, soon I may have enough to buy a couple store-bought items.

With schoolwork and earning money, I don't have much time for my art. But it's a small price to pay for my transformation.

Slowly, I'm starting to enjoy looking at myself in the glass doors at school. I finally see someone I like in the mirror.

And now I know I've inched my way into The Glam Squad as each of the girls follows me back on Instagram and TikTok—even Amanda.

But I'm worried when the last picture is finished, I don't have a reason to stay at their table unless they ask me. I don't know what'll come next.

And Ev has been on my case about eating with her group.

"I'm glad you'll be done with them soon. I can't imagine how you can stand their incessant talking in those squeaky voices. It must drive you crazy," she laughs.

On the last day, I hand Chloe her picture. She's ecstatic and says she'll frame it and hang it in her room. But as the other girls admire the drawing, I smile and wait and wait for the next step. An invitation to stay? Anything? But they just say goodbye and leave me alone at the table.

I'm so disappointed. I really want to stay in their group. Maybe Ev is right—maybe they are just using me.

The following day I go back to my old perch near Ev's lunch table of outsiders. Nothing's changed. They're planning their next revolution. Ev always objects to some injustice in the school and the group follows her. She writes editorials for the school paper and asks students to sign petitions to incite change.

Sometimes they win, sometimes they lose. Last year, she got lunch expanded to 60 minutes from 45 minutes with a petition. I respect her dedication and spunk.

Ev smiles and sits next to me.

"I'm glad you're back, Mel. I miss seeing you at lunch."

She fills me in on her current fight to get full credit for all extracurricular school activities. Right now, athletes don't have to take gym if they don't want to and can take other classes because they get the daily required exercise at team practice. But the school excludes the marching band, the show choir and the musical theatre club. They march and dance a ton. The poms dance cheer team also gets credit for dancing, but not the drama and choir kids. It makes no sense.

Ev is working on some kind of demonstration to include all three groups and any others who can prove they get as much physical activity.

As I listen to her planning their attack, Amanda walks up to us and everyone looks up in silence and shock.

The popular people just don't come up to other lunch tables. People go to them when called. This is huge.

"Mel, I'd love you to draw our poms team. Can you come to some of our practices and performances and make some sketches?"

I can't believe it. I'm beside myself. They want me to hang out with them!

Of course, I smile and say yes and Amanda goes back to her table.

The thrill must show on my face because Ev glares at me with disdain and anger in her eyes.

"They're calling you Mel now! I call you Mel. I can't understand why you're falling for this. They're using you!" she yells.

I don't know what to say to her, so I say nothing, which makes her madder.

"You're just their mascot. They wind you up and you draw pictures of them like a monkey banging cymbals on a street corner. It's wrong!" Ev roars. "I'm going to say something to them."

"No!" I shout and grab her arm. She looks at me with a hurt in her eyes I've never seen.

"Do you actually like being with them?" she asks.

Popularity

    I shrug my shoulders and she glares at me like she's seeing straight through me and leaves with her head held low. I hope she can deal with this change in my life. She wants me to be with her friends, but I want to have her friends as well. This is my chance.

Chapter Five
Poms

Ever since Amanda invited me to the poms team practice, I've been electrified with anticipation. Beyond The Glam Squad, this gives me a chance to hang out with other popular girls in school. It's a huge opportunity to see and be seen.

The dance/cheer poms team at G.S. Horton High performs at all the football and basketball halftime shows and at school assemblies for homecoming and senior week. They are the most elite group in school and everyone loves them.

Their routines are complicated, high-energy dances complete with acrobatics and pop and hip hop moves, all synchronized to a computerized light show. Sometimes they're even accompanied by a live rock band. It's nothing short of amazing.

Popularity

As a social media influencer, Amanda raised their profile by posting videos of their performances on TikTok and YouTube. Her channel has 100,000 subscribers and her videos of the poms performances and her personal tips on style frequently go viral.

Everyone on The Glam Squad is on the team. But not everyone on the poms team is in the squad.

Amanda is often the featured dancer in the group, but she's not the captain. Rumor has it that she wanted to be the captain, but another girl named Rachel was elected by the other girls because Amanda is difficult. Rachel is nicer and the other girls voted for her because she's easier to work with. That's the rumor anyway.

I can see that. Amanda is demanding. When she wasn't picked for the captain's position, she created The Glam Squad and didn't include Rachel or anyone who supported her. Amanda insists on absolute loyalty and obedience from everyone in the group. And only she decides who gets into her squad.

I show up at practice after school and sit down on a bench. Amanda and Rachel appear to be having a heated discussion when Amanda waves me over to her.

"Rachel, this is Mel. She's the artist who will be illustrating all of us. We can put it in the yearbook," she states firmly.

Rachel looks a little miffed, but she throws a quick smile at me and huffs off to practice.

"The yearbook?" I ask Amanda.

"Absolutely. I know the head of the yearbook staff. Your stuff is good and it'll be great for the pages on the team. We can intersperse photos with the drawings. Everyone will be cooperative, I promise. It'll be great," she says. Then she abruptly runs to join the routine the rest of the team is starting.

As I watch them practice, I can't help moving a little to the beat of the music. It's obvious why they're so popular. The enthusiasm is infectious.

And I'm astonished at the level of difficulty in their dances. Every step and movement are precise, with no hand askew or foot out of place. They have to be in complete synchronicity with the music and each other.

Popularity

I admire the intense discipline and commitment to their craft and the talent to pull it off. I think any one of these girls could dance on Broadway right from high school.

Looking at them perfect their routines, I wonder how best to capture their essence in my drawings. They're constantly in a state of motion, flipping in the air and changing places as they dance on the ground.

Then it hits me. The magic is both in the spectacle and in the shimmer in the eyes and smiles of each of the 20 girls. The only way to catch lightning in a bottle is to show the lightning and the bottle separately. I need to draw pictures of each of them as they are in the routine so I can show the electricity of their performance and their individual spark.

It's going to take a lot of work, but it'll be worth it to spend more time with the glam girls and get to know these other girls better. Being known by more popular people is an advantage.

My head is still reeling from Amanda's yearbook surprise. I never dreamed I would get a featured part in the yearbook. Usually, I don't like to reveal my work, but now I'll be sharing it with the whole student body—and I am loving it.

After practice when I go home, I try to imitate some of their steps. What a disaster. I fall down a bunch of times and Ev sees me on the floor when she comes in.

"Are you trying to twist yourself into a pretzel?" she laughs.

"No, just trying a dance I saw on TikTok," I say quickly to avoid questions. I know it's lying, but after her first reaction to my involvement with the glam girls, I want to skip another confrontation.

We have a running date to watch our favorite movies together and eat pizza on Friday nights.

Ev works at a pizza place in town. Her boss is really nice—he lets her bring home a pie to her family every day she works. On Fridays, she brings it to me.

And since my mom works an extra job in a bar on weekends, so we have the whole place to ourselves.

Ev and I always have a great time together. Since we became friends, we hang out whenever we can. We're both busy. I have to work and so does she, plus she helps a lot with her brothers and sisters.

Her family has nine kids. They're all adopted from foster care, as her moms wanted to create a nice home environment for abused children of drug addict parents.

Popularity

One of her moms, Janis, was addicted to opioids. She was a college volleyball star and an Olympian, but she got hurt and became hooked.

Ev says her other mom, Lucy, was her social worker and helped her quit. They both saw so many people destroyed by drugs, now they devote their lives to helping abandoned kids of addicts get a break.

She told me she was seven when her moms found her crying in a dark closet. Her "birth woman," as she calls her, died from a drug overdose.

Ev doesn't like to talk about it much, but she once told me her birth woman used to lock her in a small dark closet for hours when she did drugs with whoever was around and didn't feed her while they were binging. I can't imagine having to go through all that. Maybe that's what makes her so ferociously protective of others.

Friday nights are fun. I look forward to it every week.

"I brought my guitar. Instead of a movie, I thought we could sing and play music," she says.

I'm a horrible singer and I can't sing a note on key, but I love music. All I can usually manage is jumping up and down or pretending to dance while screeching out the words into my hairbrush. She doesn't care how bad I am, so it's still fun. She's the best.

Ev plays a fantastic guitar and even writes songs and poems. She hopes to get a rock band together someday and make it big. She tries to get me to play an instrument, but I have no skills with music. My talents are with art. I always tell her someday I'll draw the covers for her songs.

I envy people with talent and courage like Ev and the poms team. They can really put themselves out there and perform in front of people without hesitation.

That's not me. I just made the leap of showing people my work, which is a really big deal. I'm glad art is a solo gig where I can work by myself and express what comes into my mind in silence.

Chapter Six
The Game

It's my first high school football game and I get to be front and center for the action, sitting on the bench.

Even though I'm a sophomore, I've never entered the football stadium before. I don't particularly like sports, so there was no reason to be there... until now.

But I have another problem. The football games are on Friday nights, the same as my standing get-together with Ev. I'm afraid to tell her. She hates the glam girls and I know her reaction will be harsh.

"Ev, with this new assignment to illustrate the poms, I need to be at every Friday night football game. Can we do our pizza and movie night on Saturday?" I ask, bracing for the reply.

She doesn't yell or sling verbal mud at the squad or the poms team. She just looks down.

"I can't Saturday. That's date night for the moms and I need to watch the kids," she says somberly.

Now I feel worse. I'm taking away our friend time so I can be with my new friends. If she threw a fit, I almost think I would feel better. Anger I can take, but sadness and disappointment are a killer.

"I know, what if you came with me to the game? We could come back to my house afterward and still have our overnight," I say, expecting to be turned down in one sweeping blow.

She pauses for a minute and smiles at me with a sly look in her eyes.

"Sure, let's go watch the game," she says.

That look makes me feel she's up to something. Ev can be unpredictable. I don't know if she'll try to stage some protest or show up in a crazy outfit just to irritate the popular girls. But she's my friend and I owe this to her. I guess I'll just have to trust her and hope for the best.

Friday night came quickly. As is my new routine, I change my clothes several times. I need to be warmer for the night air, but I want to look like I belong.

Popularity

With Ashley's help, I've channeled my artistic vision into my clothing adding flourishes to make it custom and stylish.

I decide on my black jean jacket with rainbow glitter on the pockets and the new jeans I bedazzled with silver studs on the legs. And I found a cadet hat at Goodwill. Adding the jeweled pin my mom gave me makes it look both vintage and hip. I look good.

My mom takes Ev and me to the football game before work and one of Ev's moms will drop us back at my house afterward.

I hold my breath when we park in front of Ev's house, as I'm afraid of what she plans for the night. But she gets in the car looking like she usually does, so I'm relieved.

Her hair is a little extra spiky and bright pink and blue. And she's wearing ripped jeans and motorcycle gloves with the fingers cut off. She has a style all her own. To me, it says cool. Something I'd never have the guts to do.

When we get to the stadium, I show a special pass so we can go to the bench by the field. Sitting there, I marvel at the scene. We're right in the action next to the field surrounded by the poms girls and are in front of the football team. It's exciting.

The crowd is cheering on the team, echoing their joys and sorrows with each play. And the team perseveres and continues to go out there. It seems like they're really taking a beating, smashing up against other players and getting tackled to the ground.

But it's a real jolt when the quarterback throws a long pass and the receiver catches it and runs for a touchdown or when the kicker kicks the ball through on the posts on the field, the crowd erupts. It's easy to get caught up in the thrill of the game. Even Ev seems interested as she sits quietly watching and joins in the cheers.

It takes a lot of different kinds of talents to play this game. I never realized how complex it is. I wonder if they really like the game or if they do it for the admiration of the crowd.

It's an interesting exchange. The crowd revels in the game and maybe the players enjoy their enthusiasm too. I know what it's like to worship and envy others. I think that's what the crowd does. They live their dreams through the players. I don't know if the team craves their applause, but I know that feeling too. I love my art—it's a part of me as much as my arm or leg. But since I started to show people, I realize I like the adulation and approval I get from others. It makes me feel important and special. So, I get why it happens. I can appreciate that.

Ev appears to be enjoying herself. I'm proud of her. I know how she feels about the establishment athletes, who she believes rule the school. Maybe she's only doing this for me, but I'm grateful.

It's finally halftime and the poms will take the field to perform. Their high-energy techno music and light shows start, and the audience goes wild and jumps to their feet when the announcer introduces the team. The poms are very popular with the crowd, which claps and cheers at every move the girls make. It's sensational.

I begin to scribble wildly, flipping the pages of my sketchbook like a torrent of wind is blowing them. I want to capture the crowd's reaction too. That's something I didn't factor in before, but it's a vital part of the relationship between a performer and fans.

Listening to the echoing clapping from the stands beating the time of the music, I understand why these girls love to perform. The adoration and praise are intoxicating.

Their poms routine is impeccable. They rock every move and land every jump. Nice to see all their practice pays off.

After the rousing performance, we sit on the bench waiting for the game to restart when a couple football players walk by us and sneer and hiss.

I'm puzzled. What if they don't think we should sit here, like we don't belong? All the sudden I feel apprehensive and antsy in my seat, unsure I should be sitting there.

But then two other guys pass us and laugh.

"Is that hair camouflage?" one says.

"Yeah, like a gender reveal, you don't know if you're a girl or a boy," another laughs, pointing at Ev and they walk to the players' bench.

I feel sick, as though someone punched me in the stomach. How could they be that mean? Is her hair that offensive to their sensibilities that they need to object so strongly?

Then I get mad. Who are they to pass judgment on her hair? What are they, the hair police?

I glance over at Ev and she's completely unaffected, like it bounces right off of her shield of armor that repels stupidity.

"I'm so sorry you had to hear that. They are completely wrong." I squeeze her hand to give my support.

"Those idiots don't sting me. I know they're too dumb to understand that their hostility to me is really a reflection of their own insecurities." She laughs, barely blinking an eye.

Wow. I envy her strength. I always worry what people think of me and she never cares.

"You're so brave," I say.

"Funny, I don't see it as being brave; I see it as being me. I think it's braver to spike my hair and dye it different colors. That's a choice I made, because I like it. I don't choose to be gay, it's who I am," she says.

"I wish other people saw it that way," I reply.

"I do too," she says. "But I don't spend one ounce of my brainpower trying to figure out what goes on in the vast dark and empty recesses of their minds. It's just not worth my time."

All I can do is I shake my head in frustration. Even if it doesn't bother her, it still upsets me. And it distracts me so much, I don't even notice the girls come back to the bench after their routine.

"Did you draw those tonight?" Amanda says, looking down at my sketchbook.

"Yes."

"I like them. Keep it up," she says and sits down on the other side of the bench.

Strange how that single bit of praise changes my mood and lifts me as if I'm floating above the bench on a cloud of acclaim. The attraction to compliments is almost like a drug. But I have to admit, I like it.

After the game, Ev's mom picks us up and drops us off at my house. It's too late for pizza, but we eat some popcorn and other junk food. I'm too wired from the game to watch a movie, so I suggest we turn the music up and sing and dance.

"I'm starting to understand why people like to perform. I didn't get it before, but now I see the allure. It must feel great to have thousands of adoring fans shouting out your name and loving your music," I say.

"Yeah, I think it's a rush. But for me, I'm not in it for the applause. When I play the guitar, I'm amazed at what I

Popularity

can do. That sound is coming out of me. I guess it's the same for you and your art," Ev adds.

I nod, but I don't know if I agree. While I love to express what I'm feeling with my art, I think I like the approval even more.

Chapter Seven
Homecoming Queen

I'm starting to get into the routine of the football games. After the surprising animation of the crowd to the team wore off, I'm able to concentrate more on the electric energy of the poms team and their dynamic performances. Between the poms practices and the football games, I fill my sketchbook with drawings of the girls in various action movements.

And I can tell I feel more comfortable now. I'm still in complete awe of all of them, but I'm not as starry-eyed anymore. And I think they're used to me too. They sit and talk to me at practices. And many of the girls even say hello to me when they see me in the hallway. That's a wonderful feeling of acceptance and friendship. They see me.

Every time it happens, I sense a glow about me. I'm a little more confident. I stand up a little straighter and raise my head when I walk down the hallway. Being around the popular girls given me so much. I finally can see myself as a real member of their team.

At practice one day, Amanda asks to look at my illustrations.

I give her my sketchbook and she stares at them in stillness, without speaking or giving even one facial expression.

My heart is beginning to race and beads of sweat are starting to seep out on my forehead. Maybe she doesn't like them.

Time warps, elapsing a millisecond for each minute as I worry everything could slip away in a second.

"These are good. You've captured something radiant about the team. But maybe a few tweaks could make them stellar," she says in a dispassionate way.

She suggests a different color here and points out another possible angle there. It isn't too different and some of her ideas are good, so I'm happy to oblige.

"Now I have another job for you, if you're willing. I'm running for homecoming queen and I want you to draw some posters of me that will knock out my competition. I want the student body to see all sides of Amanda. Please say yes and we'll get together after practice. I'd love to take you for a burger, so we can talk privately," she says.

I get to have a private dinner with Amanda? Ah, yes!

I smile and nod in eager agreement and excitedly text my mom to tell her I'll be home later.

After practice, Amanda drives us to the local burger joint, Stars. I've never been in a car with a teen driver before, only adults. Amanda is a senior and her car is a beautiful silver metallic convertible her dad bought her. It's so sleek with gray leather bucket seats so comfortable, you just sink into them. As I sit there with the music blaring and the wind blowing through my hair, I think I know what cool is now. Everyone's ogling the car as we ride by. I feel envied. It's transcendent.

At Stars, I see the most popular kids in school eating and having a good time. Amanda struts down the aisle to a table as everyone watches, with me toddling behind her. I can't believe this is my life now.

She orders burgers, fries and Cokes and shows me some ideas she has for her posters.

Her ideas are smart and her drawings are surprisingly decent. She definitely has some talent for more than just dance.

"I want all the students to see me for everything I am, not just the most popular girl in school. We can show them me as a budding entrepreneur, a social media influencer and an academic. I have a very high GPA. I'm having some videos made, but I really need the posters to make everything pop," she explains.

I scribble down her ideas and relish in my position. I've become the group's go-to person for art. The other girls are the experts in clothing, hair, fashion and music. I'm the art girl in the group. I'll take it.

A week later, the dean announces the homecoming nominations will be made at the typical rally before the football game.

Ev has been going with me nearly every Friday, so we've become fixtures on the poms bench.

To kick off the event, Trina, a pom who graduated last year, returns with her homecoming queen tiara accompanied by the princess court from last year waving from a float touring around the football stadium. Amanda and Rachel are both former princesses and are vying for queen this year.

"You notice most of the girls up there are wearing pom uniforms," Ev says.

"Well, yeah. They're the most popular girls in school. Of course they're going to be elected. Don't they look beautiful up there?" I say.

As Amanda and Rachel are both seniors and very popular, they will be equal competitors in the homecoming queen race. Most students look up to them, so Amanda's right to try something different to tip the scales to her advantage.

I start to sketch a picture of the old homecoming court, but Ev grabs my arm in excitement.

"Wait for it," she says.

The announcer reads the candidates for homecoming queen this year, Rachel Barnes, Amanda Crawford and Evelyn Glen-Marks.

I'm in complete shock my head swiftly spins to meet Ev's satisfied grin.

Popularity

"Isn't it great? I'll show everyone you don't have to be a member of the twaddle troupe to run." Ev smiles, pleased by her decision.

"Of course, anyone can run, but are you sure you want to try this? You always say it's such a stupid popularity contest," I ask her, still baffled by the announcement.

"That's exactly why I should run. It gives everyone in school someone else to choose, not just the poms girls and The Glam Squad. A real person," she explains.

I just nod. I don't want to tell her that she doesn't have a chance and she's wasting her time.

"And you can help me make some cool posters to put around school," Ev smiles.

I panic the instant the words leave her mouth. I already promised Amanda I would do her posters. Would that be fair? But I can't turn Ev down either. Maybe I can make the posters totally different so no one will know?

The next day, Ev gathers her lunch group together to discuss strategies to win. They're all enthusiastically on board, yelling ideas about how they can beat the perfect princesses.

They brainstorm concepts to show Ev as the alternative candidate. Instead of voting for the beautiful people, they can vote for someone just like them.

"Vote for Ev—she's like you; vote for one of your own; and Vote for change—a regular for homecoming queen." Those are their poster ideas.

The only problem is, it'll never work. For their queen, people want someone they can look up to and place on a pedestal, not someone just like them. They vote for someone they want to be like, but know they'll never achieve.

I know Ev has no chance, but I also know it doesn't mean anything to her, so she won't care if she loses. To Ev, this is a statement on social cues. But to Amanda, this is revenge against Rachel and affirmation of her place in the school, on the poms team and as head of The Glam Squad. Her popularity is her identity, her life. It means everything to her. She would be crushed if she didn't win.

I have to help her, but I have to help Ev too. I don't have a choice. I guess I'll need to be a secret double agent. Luckily, their campaigns are very different. I just have to be careful I don't alienate either one.

But should I tell them I'm making posters for both of them? Amanda won't be threatened by Ev. She knows her competition is Rachel. But maybe Amanda will think I'm disloyal. She demands complete devotion.

No, it'll have to be a secret.

I'm in the middle. It's like balancing on top of two neighbors' fences. I can put one foot on one side and one on the other side, but one false move and I'll fall right in the middle. And it's gonna hurt.

I get to work right away on the posters. Amanda shows me her videos and I sketch her sitting in her car with her phone in her hand and another drawing of her wearing sparkly fake glasses and a lab coat on to show she's smart.

They're a little silly, but inventive and part of a strategy. Rachel's posters are pretty typical and not as inventive as either Ev or Amanda. They're pink with little silver pom-poms on them that say "Vote for Rachel for Homecoming Queen." I hate to be mean, but there's no thought or innovation behind them—pure vanilla.

Ev's posters make a statement. "Vote for Yourself." "Vote for the Anonymous." "Vote for Everyone." "Vote for the Underdog." And they say Ev for Homecoming Queen with her name at the bottom and a cool logo I made of her spiky color hair. People may not recognize her name, but they know the girl with the rainbow-colored spiky hair. It's clever.

So far, I'm getting away with it. At first, I thought my signature style would be obvious on Amanda's posters, and Ev would see right through me. But Amanda kept changing them so much, they don't even look like my work. A suggestion here, a change there—she's making them her own. But I don't care—she knows what she likes and I just like being a part of her team.

And spending all this time with Amanda elevates my status in the group even more. I think I've cemented my place in the squad. They ask me to go out with them after practice for food and iced coffee. Alyssa is giving me a makeover and I'm bedazzling with Ashley. And the glam girls are even getting me a date for the homecoming dance.

My social media presence has picked up too. I don't post much, just some pictures, but I like everything they post and they like my posts, which has increased my followers.

Many of the squad girls have huge social media followings for their dance routine videos and makeup and clothing videos. Ashley and I did a video of adding bling to some jeans and it got a lot of views. And Alyssa did a video of my makeover. Since the post, more kids at school are saying hi to me in the halls and complimenting me on my look. I am no longer invisible.

Amanda is a guru at social media. She encourages me to post about drawing with tips and tricks or just videos of me drawing. I'm going to try it. If I step up my posts and videos, I can get more followers and be noticed even more.

Her campaign videos are racking up huge likes and most have gone viral. She has some of the squad cheering "Amanda for Queen." But most of her videos are just her talking to the camera in the coffee shop, stores and the burger joint, plus a few with her driving and talking to the camera.

I like the ones where she talks about herself. I'm not a fan of the ones where she trashes Rachel. In one video, it shows The Glam Squad acting like they're secretly being filmed without their knowledge, criticizing Rachel's hair, clothes, boyfriend, everything. Amanda wasn't in the video, but had another kid post it to emphasize the hidden camera nature of the smack down.

When the video goes up, she brilliantly acts like she's shocked and embarrassed that they would say those things. It worked. The insulting information about Rachel got out and it looked unintentional, so no one blamed the glam girls or Amanda.

I think it's mean. I've been on the receiving end of bullying, teasing and snickers a lot in my life. It starts with people saying my hair is weird or I'm weird. Then my clothes aren't fancy enough; I don't live in the right neighborhood; I don't have a father; and my mother doesn't make a lot of money or have a high-profile job. I mean, what does it all matter anyway?

That's why I created my natural cloak of invisibility. If no one notices you, they can't bully you. I'm glad those days are behind me and I can shine in the sun.

But still, I just never understand why people try to prop themselves up by standing on another's back. Why can't everyone just be themselves and let everyone else be themselves too?

I guess all is fair in an election campaign, right? I don't know. I feel bad for Rachel.

Chapter Eight
Glam Mel

The homecoming queen campaign is heating up with posters all over the school and Amanda's video push. The rumor mill is buzzing and, as predicted, it's a two-way race between Rachel and Amanda, with Ev flying under the radar with all but a few loyal followers. She's really trying, constantly walking around school talking about changing the status quo.

"There are more of us than there are of the pretty people. Crown your queen from the unknown ranks," she declares at lunchtime, standing on the table.

Sporting a different hair color every other day, Ev sends out videos on Instagram and TikTok about elevating the little guy and overthrowing the popular people, again shouting "there are more of us than of them!" as a tagline.

She talks about the perils of popularity and confesses how much easier it is to be one of the many instead of glittering in the limelight of the exalted few who must maintain their pedestal status.

I think some of her message is directed at me, but it's a clever concept and Ev is getting some attention—maybe too much.

As she begins to gain a little ground, some of the football players and other guys in the popular crowd have taken offense at their status symbol group being put on the defense.

They vandalize her posters with paint splotches and less inventive black marker art.

Ev shrugs it off. Haters gonna hate. But the literal smear campaign is beginning to get more personal.

This morning, many of her posters are marked "Queen or King???" under her name in black marker.

It really upset me. Homecoming queen has nothing to do with someone being gay.

I don't want her or anyone else to see the marred hate posters, so I go around the school taking them down as fast as I can when Ev catches me.

"Keep them up," she says calmly, taking them from my hand.

"But they're vile and stupid," I insist.

"Mel, I'm not new to being gay. I have gay moms too. This kind of thing's going to happen. Let it. Types of hate like this make them look worse than me. I'm not hiding who I am. I celebrate it," she says.

I guess she's right. People need to see each other for what they are. So, we put the posters back up, as is.

I respect her attitude and her ideals, but I worry it won't stop at just defacing posters. Sometimes when you ignore bullies, they just go away. But other times, they keep coming.

Unfortunately, these goons don't let up. They egged her house in a late-night raid. I get a picture text when I wake up in the morning and ride over there to help Ev, her moms and her brothers and sisters wash it off.

When I get there, they're already washing it off like it's just any other task.

"I'm so sorry. It's just so wrong. Isn't there a way to report this?" I say.

"Let it be. The more interest you give them, the more they feed on it. Just ignore it," Ev says and throws a bucket of watery soap against the wall.

"Why do these jerks keep doing this?" I ask Ev's moms, Janis and Lucy.

"It's about fear," Lucy says. "They're afraid of what they don't know. Anyone different is hard to understand."

"You're too nice, Lucy," Janis challenges. "I think it's about control. They want the status quo. New means change. And people like this want everything to be as it is. They want life to be the same as it always was with everyone believing the same way they do. The more different people there are, the less their way of life dominates. That scares them."

"That's dumb. If there was only one color on my palette, my art would look dull. It's only interesting with different colors, style and textures. I wish they spent less time worrying about change and more being kind," I say.

"Me too," Janis agrees.

We work through the day to clean the house, with everyone eventually squirting each other. I like coming here. Their house is chaotic, but loving.

As an only child, I can only take the big family life in small doses; it's a little loud. But it's nice to have a built-in team or group whenever you need it.

It's such a shame people like those bullies are so narrowminded. I think Lucy and Janis are amazing. They didn't have to take all these kids in, but they did.

All the bullies see are differences and don't even try to see them for what they are—just a wonderful family.

Ev and her moms tell me to let it go, but I just feel bad for them and I want to do something. So, I talk to Amanda about it when they have a break at poms practice, thinking she could encourage the guys to quit.

"Don't worry about it. They're just dumb boys. Everything to them is physical. They'll wear themselves out and move on to the next thing," she says dismissively.

"Speaking of boys, the girls found you a date for the dance. More to come," she smiles and runs off to start another routine.

In an instant, my mood changes. I perk up in excitement. Suddenly, I'm Cinderella going to the ball and it's all I can think about.

Later that night, I get a text.

"See the girls tomorrow at lunch for details about your date," Amanda texts.

I can't wait until tomorrow. I wonder what he'll be like. I have so many questions. Is he tall or short, muscular or slim? What's he into—sports, academics, maybe even music and art? That's too much to hope for. I can't actually believe I'm going to a dance… with a date.

All night I search through the internet for styles and dress ideas. And I scroll through IG for the chatter about the dance. #hortonhomecoming. It's all incredible.

I've been trying to eat lunch with Ev's crowd and then spend time after practice with the glam girls to perfect my tightrope balancing act in both worlds.

But today, I can't wait to find out about my date, so I eat with the glam girls to get the scoop.

"His name is Taylor and he's really fresh," Alyssa says.

"You'll like him. I think he's smart and creative, like you," Ashley says.

"But more importantly, he's nice to look at," Brittany says and shows me a picture on her phone. "Your pictures will be great."

I look at the picture and linger. He has a kind face and nice eyes. I like that.

"Don't worry, we'll help you with everything you need to get ready," Alyssa says.

"We all have closets full of designer dresses that we've worn before - you can have your choice," Amanda offers.

I've never been more excited in my life. Not once did I think I would ever go to a dance with a date and wear a beautiful designer dress. It's a fairy tale coming true.

"And we have one more thing for you," Amanda says and hands me a pink and purple glittery notecard labeled "The Glam Squad Rules." My own personal copy of the 10 coveted Glam Squad commandments.

1. Always look fabulous
2. Always wear lipstick and gloss
3. Never go out in public without full makeup, hair and fashion forward coordinated outfit
4. Never let anyone else rise above you
5. Always date someone popular
6. Never be seen with undesirables
7. Always believe in yourself
8. Always stay online and connected
9. Always support the squad
10. Never betray the squad

This is it. I feel like a rocket ship bounding through the air to the stars, soaring to new heights. I'm ready. It's official. I'm part of the squad now.

And for the first time, when they leave, I walk in line with them.

On the way to class, I happily stroll down the halls, reading the rules over and over to memorize them, when Ev sneaks up on me.

"Missed you at lunch today. Did you have business with the twaddles?" She laughs and sees the shiny card in my hand.

"Oh, no, don't tell me you're in with them now." She looks at me with a crinkled brow of disbelief. That's her go-to face when she questions me.

"It's a real honor to be accepted. I'm excited," I say.

"You know they're treating you like a pet, a novelty. When they're done with you, they'll leave you behind. They don't care about you," Ev says, with a sharp tone.

"I know I'm not like them. I'm fully aware that they could be using me, but I'm using them too. I just want to be part of their world. They're already changing my life. I actually have a date for homecoming and will wear a beautiful dress," I say.

"Look at that list!" She grabs it out of my hand. "That's a lot of work to keep sitting next to the throne. You obviously haven't been listening to my campaign," she accuses.

"I like it. I get something and I give them something. What's the harm?" I object.

"For your sake, I hope there is no harm." Ev hands the card back to me and walks away.

Her words echo in my head all day, but I feel good about myself for the first time in my life. When I look in the mirror, I no longer see boring old Melinda. I see Mel. I like Mel. I want to be her forever.

I decide not to let Ev dampen my spirits. After poms practice today, I'm going on a closet tour to try on dresses. This is the life I've always wanted.

Ashley, Chloe, Brittany, Alyssa and I squeeze into Alyssa's open air white and gold trimmed Jeep. Amanda isn't with us, as she had her last day of campaign videos to film. She'll meet us at her house later.

Being in a car with other teen girls is like being in a music video. Everyone's on their phones, talking at the same time and the music is super loud with several manes of long hair flapping in the breeze. It's fun. I like it.

"Where should we go first?" Brittany asks.

"Oh, we can't go to my house. The house painters are there. My mom redecorates all the time," Ashley says.

"My house is closest—we can go there first," Chloe says.

While I've hung out with the glam girls at their various haunts after practice, I've never been to any of their homes. As we drive up through the entrance gate, I feel like I'm arriving at a fancy hotel. Chloe's house is an enormous sleek white block design with tall contemporary windows that seem to reach up to the sky.

And when we walk inside, I'm dumbfounded by the heights of the clean white and glass walls. It's just like the chic modern designs you see in architectural posts online.

As I rubberneck everything in my path, the other girls climb the glass and silver metal stairs to Chloe's bedroom without even looking. It's nothing they haven't seen before.

Her bedroom looks as big as my whole house. Her white canopied bed sits on a fluffy white rug atop the gleaming glossy gray tile floors. The glow of a light shines up from moldings on the walls. And there's a giant TV and a refrigerator and microwave in her room. She makes popcorn and offers everyone diet sodas.

Along one wall, a huge glass case displays all her gymnastics trophies and ribbons, like a shrine to her success.

I peek in her bathroom and see a walk-in shower and a tub with a waterfall cascading down into the drain. This isn't a bedroom—it's a luxury suite.

Chloe opens the closet door and a succession of lights come on automatically, shining on the compartments of shoes, jewelry, sunglasses and clothes. Another smaller light hangs in the middle over the square white leather ottoman. As everyone sits on the big ottoman, Chloe motions over to me.

In one corner of the closet is a sliding glass door with all the dresses behind it. It's like I'm gazing through a store window awed by all the sparkle and gleam of the shimmering party dresses.

"Help yourself. Try on anything." She smiles and plops down on the floor.

"Don't worry, if anything doesn't fit—I can make anything work!" Ashley yells out and Chloe nods in approval.

I'm frozen. For a moment, it's like I'm afraid to move for fear it'll all disappear, and I'll wake up from a dream. Plus, I don't know what I'm doing. I have no idea what dress would be good. I just stand there in a panicked daze and Ashley jumps up and grabs a few options for me.

I try on dress after dress. I'm not even glancing at a mirror, but I trust the girls on what looks good on me or not. They have much more experience with this. With thumbs up on two possibilities, I gather them and in a shot, we're back in the Jeep on the way to Brittany's house.

When we arrive, a huge iron gate opens from the street onto a winding path lined with bushes, trees and flowers. I smile and wonder if she lives next to an arboretum as I view the manicured gardens. Then we pull into a beautiful cobblestone courtyard with a fountain in the middle and get out of the car.

Brittany opens an iron gate entry and we follow her into a courtyard. I circle around in amazement, taking in the view of the Spanish-style casa surrounding me with curved arched wooden doors and small iron balconies at each window.

"Sorry, the elevator's being repaired, so we need to walk up to my floor," she says.

Popularity

Her floor? Her bedroom is a floor?

Brittany's floor is composed of a series of rooms at the top of the house. There's a TV and game room, bedroom, bath, closet, kitchenette and outdoor balcony overlooking the pool. The size is staggering. It's a whole house, just for her.

It's cozier than Chloe's sleek white and glass house with the warmer brown and terra cotta colors, but I'm surprised it doesn't look a lot like Brittany. The room has a lot of iron and muted colors, just like the house—definitely not the floral-loving Brittany I see at school.

We open the closet doors and all I can see is Brittany. Lining the big walk-in closet are racks of colorful floral clothes with shelves of multi-colored hats, sunglasses and shoes. This time, Brittany took out some dresses from her store-like closet for me to try on. I think they realize that I'm completely out of my element. I try on some more dresses, the girls short-list a few and we're off again. By this time, I'm surrounded by hanging bags of glitter, glitz and sequins. I feel like a rock star.

Then on to Alyssa's beach house. Finally, I picture a modest home on the beautiful beach with the waves coursing on the shore. But as the Jeep rises up and up a mountaintop to the heavens, I see a stately cliff-side mansion overlooking the beach. A mansion built on the side of a cliff is something to be seen.

As we enter through the towering glass front door I feel like a doll inside a dream house.

"Welcome to Mountain's Peak, Mel," she says and ushers us into the foyer. The first thing I see through the wall of windows is the sky above and the roaring ocean below, like a painted canvas in all its beauty.

I'm nearly breathless standing in awe of the view.

"Come on, Mel, more to see," Alyssa says, waving me to follow her.

On our way to her bedroom, we pass through the theatre screening room.

"Wow, this place is amazing! It looks just like a regular movie theatre. I've heard of movie business people having fancy private screening rooms in their homes.

"It must be exciting to have parents in the movie business," I say, marveling at the enormous screen towering above my head and the reclining red leather seats with snack and cup holders in each arm.

Popularity

"I wish. They're just boring old lawyers. I really like movies, so they built this room. We have surround sound and a real soda fountain and popcorn maker too."

On the other side of the movie theatre is Alyssa's bedroom, all decked out in her signature glittering gold walls and crisp white furniture everywhere. And in true Alyssa style, the walls are decorated with life-size pictures of herself in various modeling poses.

Her closet had white drawers and doors, but the luminous gold lighting reflected everything to look like glitter.

I begin to see how this kind of life is normal to them. All the homes are so luxurious, and their enormous closets filled with beautiful clothes. Maybe being surrounded by so many lovely things made them take it for granted.

Again, I try on dresses Alyssa selects as the girls quickly weigh in with yeas or nays and back down the mountain we went nearly as quickly as we came. It's almost becoming a routine.

Our last stop is Amanda's house. As we pass through the automatic iron scrolled gates, I hear rushing water and see a giant waterfall right in front of the golden mansion. In my head, this is what a real a movie star's home looks like... Old Hollywood glamor.

We knock on the glistening gold front door and a butler leads us into a tan marble foyer with an enormous crystal chandelier glistening in the sun's light on the curving grand staircase like I saw in an old movie, *Gone with the Wind*.

Amanda comes sauntering down the stairs like Scarlett O'Hara. I might be living in a dream.

She tours us through the house to her wing. Of course, Amanda has her "own wing."

Amanda says the house was built in the 1930s by a head of a studio and his socialite wife, so they had a grand ballroom and huge outdoor pool area where they entertained movie stars.

Amanda's wing includes her own sitting area and recreation room with a balcony overlooking the pool.

Her bedroom matches the home and Amanda, as the grandeur of both fits her to a tee. It's gorgeous with a big silver mirrored headboard on slightly the elevated bed and gray satin bedspread above a clean white carpet sculpted in squares on the floor. All the furniture is silver, with mirrors sparkling in the sun.

Popularity

Her vast closet makes the others look like cubbyholes. We enter to see mirrors all around with no doors or shelves, and she speaks into her phone and the closet comes to life. A shoe rack twirls around, displaying hundreds of pairs of shoes in all shapes and colors. Drawers pop open, displaying jewelry and sunglasses. And rotating racks of clothes suddenly produce her formalwear. It's amazing.

She selects two beautiful dresses and some shoes and hands them to me without any input from the other girls.

"Here you go. You don't need to try them on," she says and I shake my head in agreement.

Amanda never needs anyone's advice. I guess that's why she's the leader of the glam girls.

Just like that, we're back out the door and on our way back to my house.

As we ride home, my mind boggles at seeing all these incredible homes. It's like I've just been in a whirlwind of a world I can't comprehend. What can these people do to make this much money?

And it truly astonishes me that none of them seems fazed by the grandeur of the homes. I hope if I ever have that kind of luxury around me all the time, I won't tire of it or take it for granted.

The girls drop me at my house and I walk in with arms full of sanctioned dresses and matching shoes to select. I immediately plop on my couch, surrounded by glittering dresses. I truthfully had no idea what I brought home, only a big mound of fluff, frill and bling.

I told myself I would go through every dress methodically to decide on one, but for right now, I need a breather.

After that exhausting trip through the lifestyles of the rich and famous, I look around my house.

I see the walls my mom and I painted and repainted when we changed our minds about the color. The eclectic furniture and knickknacks we searched far and wide for at estate sales, thrift stores and flea markets to decorate the house with together. And all the crazy DIY projects we had a blast completing to make our home look bohemian, playful and cool. We'd look them up on YouTube. Sometimes they worked and at times, they were a disaster, but always fun. It's tiny, cozy and filled with personality and memories. It's home to me and I wouldn't have it any other way.

Chapter Nine
The Dance

The next day, I lay out all the dresses and shoes to try them on by myself. This time, I actually need to look at them. I don't have a full-length mirror, since I never needed one before, so I place a chair in front of our bathroom mirror to see more of the dresses when I stand on it.

The first one is a full-length sleek emerald satin dress with choker neckline and open back from Amanda. It is so her—powerful, glamourous and a little dangerous.

As I see my reflection, I let out a chuckle. I'm obviously kidding myself. No one will believe me in this dress. It's beautiful and shines in the light, but on me, it looks like a costume, like I'm pretending to be someone I'm not.

The other dress Amanda gave me is short with sparkly gray fabric. Another choker neckline and open shoulders and long flowing translucent sleeves. I take a quick look in the mirror and laugh again. It's ridiculous. I look like a little girl wearing my mother's dress. It's just too sophisticated for me.

I really want to wear one of Amanda's dresses, but she'll understand. *Teen Vogue* would say she's chic and urbane. She's on a different level.

Next up are Brittany's dresses. I have little hope for these, as she is much curvier than I am.

The first one is an amethyst color with a little iridescence. It's pretty, but when I put it on, it slumps at the top over my small chest. Add in my frizzy and voluminous hair and I resemble a cartoon.

If I wore this, I'd have to stuff two entire rolls of toilet paper to make it fit. I'd never do that. Even the thought is too depressing.

Out of respect, I try the other one on. It's even worse. It's a sparkly lime color, but I'd need two paper towel rolls this time. I'm not sure what the girls were thinking.

When I take it off, I see the tag still on it. It says $10,000. I don't know what's more shocking, the price or that she spent that much money and never wore it.

Alyssa's dresses, one gold and white are cute. The gold one has a satin sheen that makes it look like pure liquid gold. But it's long and Alyssa's much taller than me. So I know it's not going to work. I pull it up in front of me and note the sea of liquid gold on the floor. Plus, I'm just not that chic to pull off a dress that looks like an Oscar.

The other white one is short with a halter strap and some silver rhinestones. I really like this one, but when I try it on, I keep having to wave the feathers at the bustline out of my face. And after a few sneezes, I put that one in the "I don't know/maybe" pile. I can't keep sneezing all night, but it does fit and on me, the length is at the knees, which is more comfortable for me. I can't imagine how short it is on Alyssa.

The last two are Chloe's. I have the most hope for these as she also has a petite physique, and I'm quickly running out of prospects. After all, I have to wear one of these dresses. I can't afford a glamourous dress and it would be ungrateful not to wear one I borrowed, since the squad is being so generous.

The dresses are both blue, my favorite color. In paints, blue can transform so many other colors into richer versions of themselves. Like when mixed with red, it becomes blue and with yellow, it becomes green. It even tones orange down into rust or umber.

The first one is a pretty cornflower blue with a strapless V-shaped neckline. The "V" could have been too revealing on some girls my age, but with my flat chest, it's fine. But then I see the label—Vera Wang—and I shiver in terror and carefully take it off and lay it on the bed.

It's an option, but I think I would be too scared to wear such an expensive dress. I'd walk around all night like a stiff, terrified to spill something on it, tear it, or even muss it. Vera Wang is a top designer. Too rich for me. But it fits, so I need to put it in the maybe pile.

Since this is my first dance, with a date for the first time, I'm going to be so nervous. I'm already scared just thinking about it. I'm just not sure I can take any chance that something may happen to the dress. I don't think I could look the girls in the face if I ruined an expensive designer dress. I could never replace it.

I look at the label on the next dress before I even pick it up. I don't recognize the name, so I put it on.

It's a beautiful deep royal blue with a straight neckline and straps, but it's a short dress with a side slit. With Chloe's muscular tanned legs, it may look good, but my pale skin and normal legs won't have the same effect. And when I sit down on my bed, I panic looking down at the new location of the slit. No. I don't need to show everything below my skirt off before its due date.

    I stare at all the spectacular dresses strewn across my bed and feel like Goldilocks. This one's too big, that one's too small, too everything. Nothing is right. But one has to work.

    I may have to face the fact that I don't belong in this circle. These girls are on a different plane of existence than me.

    After a few minutes of despair, I'm saved by the bell at the front door.

    "I hope it's ok I just came by, but I want to explain myself for yesterday," Ashley says with an exasperated look on her face.

    "What about yesterday?" I ask, puzzled and a little embarrassed, as I'm still in the blue slitty dress.

    "I lied about why we couldn't go to my house," she confesses with her head down. "The girls all think I'm rich like them, but I'm not. My parents are teachers and we live in a very average home. I'm not ashamed or anything, but if the girls knew I didn't have houses like them, they'd kick me out of the squad."

"No, they wouldn't," I tell her and invite her into the house. "I don't know how many people have houses like theirs, but I've never known anyone like that. Thanks for telling me. It means a lot that you trust me. I'm glad to know I'm not the only odd person out. I am a little surprised though; you always dress like you buy the best."

"Thanks. I'm lucky that I can sew and have some ideas on style. I study fashion a lot. I have to just to keep up appearances," she says.

"Since we're being honest, I don't know if I can wear any of these dresses. They're too much for me." We both laugh as I point to the slit and shake my head.

She gazes at the dress for a minute with a pensive look.

"If you want to wear it, I can make you a glittery organza skirt to go over the top. But I may have another option," she offers. She hands me a large canvas bag.

"I can't afford designer dresses, so I either rent them or make them myself. But I don't want you to think I'm holding out on you. This is my favorite. I made it."

Popularity

I open the bag and see a rainbow of pastel colors in beads and sequins. I pull it out, and it's stunning. It has rose color trim and straps and small repeating diagonal stripes of silver, teal, pink and pearl.

I'm speechless. It's perfect.

"Can I try it on now?" I ask with exuberant anticipation.

We run to my room and I change the slit dress for Ashley's pastel sequined creation. Ashley zips me up and I race to the bathroom mirror with her following behind.

"This is amazing. It really fits," I say, admiring myself.

"It fits you in every way, but maybe it's a little too short? I can add some small trim in the rose color to the bottom. I still have the fabric," she says.

When I glance down, I see what she means. It's a little short. I'm so excited, I don't even notice. In this dress I feel pretty, but I also feel like me.

On the day of the dance, my mom drops me off at Amanda's on her way to work. The girls invited me to Amanda's house to get ready and stay there after. I'm so excited.

When we pull up at Amanda's house, my mom's eyes nearly pop out of their sockets as we pull up the drive.

"I know," I laugh. "I'm glad I'm not the only one who sees it."

I return the girls' dresses and give them colored drawings of each one of them in one of the dresses. I want to show them how much their kindness means to me, even though I didn't wear their dresses.

All is forgiven, especially when I put on Ashley's dress and they ooh and ahh.

Dressing together is so much fun. Alyssa does everyone's hair and makeup, and she tames my wild beast hair better than I ever did. For once, my curls look like perfectly scalloped icing on a cake. And she complemented the dress and my pale skin with light pink blush, lip gloss and eyeshadow with a bit of brown mascara and no liner.

I look in the full-length mirror and I'm so overwhelmed with joy, but I don't want to tear up and mess my makeup. I can't believe the girl looking back at me… is me. I feel pretty, like Cinderella in a magical dream and they're all my fairy godmothers.

Popularity

When everyone's ready, we strut down the grand staircase like a pageant parade as the photographer Amanda's mother hired takes our picture.

At the bottom of the stairs, Amanda's mother and father are dressed to the nines, raising champagne glasses to us. It's so special.

The boys arrive shortly after, looking as dapper as *GQ* cover models in their tuxedos. All the guys are popular in sports or other clubs at our school and are very good looking.

The Glam girls don't really have boyfriends, they have dates, but they always come from the same pool of people. Amanda says it's important to date someone who compliments or blends with you in pictures.

Chase, Amanda's date, has a black velvet suit with white high-collar shirt and no tie. Chad's suit is dark red and very tailored for his tall slim frame. He's Chloe's date. Astin, who's going with Alyssa, wears a black alligator coat paired with a striped black and white shirt. Brent, Brittany's date, is in a red velvet tux with a black shirt.

Ryan is the only boyfriend in the group. Ashley says they've dated forever. His outfit is a twin to Amanda's father in a classic black tux and black tie.

But my favorite, hands down, is Taylor with an old-school black bowtie and cummerbund with white suit coat and black pants. It's retro and chic. Plus, since he's my date, I really want to like his suit the most. Admiring his slicked-back blond hair and blue eyes, I stand there in a frozen trance. He is the coolest version of Prince Charming.

I can't help but wonder if I have a goofy grin on my face to match my feelings inside. He's so perfect!

He walks up to me and takes my hand to put a wrist corsage on it.

"Hi, my name is Taylor," he smiles at me.

I think my knees will buckle right here, but I stand strong and thank him. That's all I can get out. I'm tongue-tied.

As we're whisked away by the photographer to take all the group and couples' pictures on the grand staircase and outside in front of the cascading waterfall.

When we're done, servers hand out hors d'oeuvres and glasses of sparkling drink with bubbles on sterling silver trays. It's all so elegant, I can't believe how lucky I am to be here.

I take a sip, but it's bitter, so I nearly spit it out. I'm able to swallow it, but it burns a little when it goes down. I thought it was sparkling cider, but it's real champagne. They're all drinking it like water, but we're underage and not allowed to drink alcohol.

It's just one sip, but it feels wrong. I stealthily move near a plant and slowly pour the rest in there a little at a time, so it seems like I'm a slow drinker. I don't want the others to think I'm a square, but just the same, I don't want to drink it.

We go outside and are greeted by a long white SUV limousine. It isn't a golden pumpkin coach; it's much better. Inside, the lights along the ceiling dance to the rhythm of the music playing.

The venue for the dance is a fancy country club with a banquet room lined in tanned marble swirls.

I definitely walked through the looking glass into a strange and wonderful world. It's extraordinary.

There are tables with all kinds of food surrounding the room and stand-up tables for eating. The high-top tables are dressed in gold sparkling cloths, cinched at the bottom with huge white ribbons.

Everyone scatters to get food, as I stand there dumfounded.

"I'd be happy to bring you a plate. Do you know what you want to eat?" Taylor asks.

Ooo. He's so sweet, but I don't want to tell him I'm too nervous and awed to digest anything, so I just say I'm not that hungry and he should go ahead without me.

I stay at a table alone, panning from left to right, scanning the room. It's a dream. Everyone from school looks so posh and beautiful.

As I see people coming back with food, though, I start to get a little hungry. To avoid the risk of a rumbling stomach at a quiet moment, I figure I better eat something.

I notice a few people with mashed potatoes in martini glasses and wander around until I find that station.

At the mashed potato bar, you can fill your glass with any toppings. The martini glass adds a stylish touch. These people think of everything.

On my way back to the table, I run into Ev. She's there with a girl named Elli.

Always true to herself, Ev is dressed in a multi-colored plaid sparkly suit and eggplant shirt with a ribbon tie to go with her dark purple Easter egg hair. She would never wear a dress, so a glittery avant-garde suit is the best option for a homecoming queen nominee. It's the most fashion-forward thing I've ever seen. I admire her unbending ability to be true to herself, regardless of the circumstance. With leather purple high tops, the outfit draws a lot of glares. It's original.

Ev's mothers rented the suit from a fancy tux place in Hollywood for the occasion. And Ev can wear those shoes every day. They're cute.

"I love your suit," I smile.

"You look nice too. I'd ask where you got that pretty dress, but I already know the answer. I saw you pull up with the other twaddles in that ridiculous limousine. With its size, it could be in two zip codes at once."

Her sharpness cut me a bit, but for now, I don't want to burst my perfect bubble tonight, so I just let it go.

"Well, I better eat this before it cools. Good luck," I say and we both leave in opposite directions.

As I walk back to the table, my heart sinks in my chest. I know she doesn't like my association with The Glam Squad, but I thought she'd be happier for me. I keep thinking once she sees I can be friends with her and the glam girls at the same time, she'll get used to the idea. But I don't know. Either way, it's a problem for another time.

After everyone eats, the music starts and people move to the dance floor.

Taylor takes my hand and we walk to the dance floor. My group goes out on the dance floor and forms a circle where everyone dances together, instead of in couples.

I've always wondered about teen dancing. The glam girls are obviously skilled, as they're almost professionals on the poms team. Even some of the guys have moves, but it seems so random. There is no symmetry or order, just sporadic movement with each person dancing to their own tune in their own singular way. But dance is an expression of art too, so it's individual and anything goes.

I don't really know how to dance, although I watch plenty of TikTok videos. But every time I try to learn a dance, it starts over. It's only 10 to 20 seconds, after all.

So, I just move my arms and feet back and sway in time with the music. And that's the funniest thing of all—I fit in perfectly. It's so strange.

Then the slow music starts and Taylor says, "Dance?"

I nod, but I am beyond nervous. I've never slow-danced with a partner before, but looking around, it's pretty simple. I put my hands on his shoulders and he puts his on my hips and we sway back and forth to the music. Easy.

After a minute, I'm in the groove and have a chance to look at him. His eyes are so close to mine that they look like reflective pools of blue water shimmering in the cascading lights, shining an array of colored stars around the room. It's nice, even romantic.

We go back to the table after a few songs to rest and wait for the big homecoming queen announcement. I voted for Amanda since I know Ev is only doing it for political reasons. It means nothing to her, but it means everything to Amanda.

She stands tall with consummate poise and confidence as they dim the lights and shine a spotlight on the stage. I watch her and wonder if she's nervous or really that sure of herself. Sometimes people have a hard shell, but they're soft inside.

I've never seen anything about Amanda to support the idea of a gooey center, but I can't believe anyone is that cool and self-assured all the time.

They dim the lights and a spotlight shines on the stage where the dean will announce the winner. I glance over at Amanda again. She's like a rock, but I'm so anxious for her; I'm like putty. I can't take the waiting and waiting and waiting, while the dean makes even a brief speech. It's torture!

"And without further ado, for this year's homecoming queen, the winner is Rachel Barnes, with Amanda Crawford and Evelyn Glen-Marks as princesses. Please come up here, girls, and take your crowned positions."

We all stare straight at each other with giant saucer eyes in shock. Amanda didn't win. I watch her, fearing an explosion of monumental proportions, but she maintains a regal poise with her head held high and marches up to the stage as a princess.

And she remains stoic as Rachel is excitedly crowned queen. I'm impressed. When they place the smaller princess tiara on her head, she has a look of pride on her face. It's obviously for show—inside she has to be gutted—but she's handling it with grace.

Ev goes up to the stage as a princess, but when they try to put the tiara on her head, she intercepts it and takes in her hands. I'm sure she doesn't want it to mess her hair. And she'd never wear a tiara. When they walk down the stairs, she puts the tiara on a smiling Elli, as they dance with the rest of the homecoming court and their dates.

I observe how majestic they all look dancing in the spotlight with the gleaming tiaras and crown, but my heart goes out to Amanda. Her campaign meant so much to her, and to lose to Rachel is a crushing blow. The pinnacle of high school popularity, to be its queen, just slipped through her fingers.

But just then, in the rotating spotlight, I see a bunch of football players walk near the dance floor in the darkness. I can't see what they're carrying, but I hold my breath, afraid of what they're up to. When the spotlight moved to Ev and Ellie, they dump a full bowl of red punch over Ev's head.

"Next time, stay out of the queen business. You're not a girl!" one yells with venom in his voice.

The music stops instantly, and everyone is stunned into silence, peering at the unexpected assault in disbelief. Suspended in time, like many others, I don't know what to do.

I feel a little tear stream from each of my eyes, and this wakes me out of my daze. I run to the floor, grabbing several linen napkins along the way to help.

Poor Ev is humiliated and angry, while Elli is wailing with embarrassment. When I get to Ev, I start to pat her down with the napkins and she pushes me.

"Get away from me, you traitor!" she screams.

"What?" I say in confusion, with more tears in my eyes.

"You're with them now. You like it. Stay with them and stay clear of me!" she yells and storms out of the room.

There I am in the spotlight holding cherry-colored napkins in my hands, paralyzed and astounded, with my heart breaking in sadness and shock. Neither my friends nor I had anything to do with the football players who attacked her. Why is she mad at me?

I drop the napkins and slowly walk back to the table, silent and hurt. Amanda and Chase are back when I arrive and everyone's talking about the incident.

"Those stupid boys—why do they have to be so dumb?" Chloe says.

"That's so uncalled for. She isn't harming anyone," Brittany chimes in.

"I'm not condoning their actions, but she likely took votes away from me and skewed the results. It's a gag to her, but still there's no reason for violence, ever," Amanda says with a curt tone.

Still in a fog of despair, I barely hear what they say, but I notice their demeanor. They feel sorry for her, but they don't seem to care a lot.

They all brush it off and immediately continue talking. The dance ends, given the attack, and everyone walks back to the limousine to go back to Amanda's.

I sit in the back with Taylor, as they're all chattering, but I still can't process the pain Ev must be feeling and the rage she wreaked on me when I didn't do anything.

Then I feel Taylor grip my hand and I gaze up at him. His eyes are thoughtful and sympathetic, reminding me I'm on my first date. So, I smile at him and resolve to fix things with Ev later.

We get to Amanda's house and everyone's excited to continue the party. Amanda's having a sleepover at her house with brunch tomorrow for everyone.

Amanda has a huge pool and hot tub, so we all change into our suits and go for a swim. There are pizzas, popcorn and chips on the pool bar with a soda machine that dispenses any kind of soda.

I see a couple of people pour alcohol in their drinks from the full bar, but I turn the other way and ignore it.

Amanda has the music blaring and everyone's eating and dancing. It's fun and playful, and several people jump into the pool. Taylor picks me up and throws me in, then jumps in next to me. I tie it into a braid to avoid massive expansion and frizz of my uncontrollable mop.

The water's a perfect temperature and a few of us toss beach balls at each other.

After we are all soaked and tired, the girls and I go to Amanda's room to change into lounge pants and T-shirts. We meet the boys back in her recreation room.

I like being around Taylor. He's nice, fun and dreamy. I want to get to know him better, so we sit and talk about school and music for a while. We don't have a lot in common, but it's a good conversation. He's smart. I like that.

Then the music turns down low and the lights go dim. I'm not sure what's going on, but Taylor takes my hand.

"Do you want to kiss a little?" he says.

I glance around the room and that's exactly what they're all doing. I'm unsure of myself, as I've never done this, but I nod with complete uncertainty and suddenly wonder if my breath stinks from the pepperoni pizza I just ate. I'm terrified, excited and curious all at the same time. It's my very first kiss.

Taylor leans toward me, but I don't move. I figure he knows what he's doing and if I move, I could mess it up. I'd probably aim my head the wrong way and we'd crash noses or something equally awkward.

He does know what to do. He tilts his head and places his lips on mine. It feels nice. His lips are soft. Then he puts his arm around me and gently pulls me closer to him. His arms are strong and his lips are locked on mine. Not knowing what to do, I push my lips against his.

As we kiss, my mind drifts off a little. I feel a strange warm feeling rush over me like warm water on a hot beach day. I can feel the butterflies in my stomach, but I also notice a calming sense of joy. I like this feeling.

Chapter Ten
High Maintenance

After the make-out session, Amanda orders the boys to their side of the house and the girls to theirs and commands everyone to get their beauty sleep. It's a big house, so everyone can be separated.

"I'm filming a video tomorrow, so I can't get bags under my eyes. None of you can afford those either," she warns.

Since the election is over, it's natural that Amanda would refocus her efforts on her influencer career. She often talks about how she can get this or that product to pay her to endorse it to her followers. She has a whole plan on how she's going to be a famous businesswoman.

I'm only a sophomore, but sometimes I wonder if I should have a plan. I don't. Maybe art school—I don't know.

Popularity

I can't sleep. As the other girls snooze their cells into beautification, my mind is racing with thoughts and feelings about my wonderful new life.

Right now, all I can focus on is high school. I always thought high school would just be a blip that I would forget and discard as I move on with my life. But now I see it all through the lens of cool sunglasses. I am a member of The Glam Squad. I have friends. I ride in fancy cars, stay in mansions and go to dances and parties. I have a glimmer of a boyfriend. This is a whole new ballgame.

When everyone awakens from their slumber, we dress and meet the boys downstairs for brunch. As with everything else, brunch in Amanda's house is done to the nines. There's more food than I've ever seen—fruit, pastries, eggs done in more ways than I can name, waffles, pancakes and several kinds of meats.

Some indulge in mimosas with fruit juice and champagne. I stick with straight juice, but I like drinking from a champagne flute. In fact, I like everything.

After brunch, Ashley offers to take me home. I know my house is on her way home, but to keep up her ruse of living in a fancy neighborhood, I fake objections that I'm taking her out of her way. She smiles at me, knowing my intention. It's our secret.

As we drive to my house in her cute convertible pink Volkswagen Bug with adorable eyelashes on the headlights, I ask her questions about the guys from the dance and party and their relationships.

"Amanda says The Glam Squad has dates, not boyfriends. Why don't the girls want boyfriends?"

"Oh, don't listen to Amanda," she laughs.

She gives me the 411 on all the guys and their relationships with the girls, like my translation dictionary for their world.

"I think Chase is more of a trophy to Amanda. He looks good in pictures and doesn't outshine her, so she likes to have him on her arm. But no, she doesn't want or like boyfriends. I don't think she really *like* likes him. But that doesn't mean the others don't have a preferred date. Chad and Chloe have been dating for about a year. They're both smart athletes. I think he'll be valedictorian this year.

"Brent and Brittany are fairly new. He used to go out with Alyssa and Astin dated Brittany, but they just seemed to stray toward the other direction and one day, they just swapped partners. I was worried there would be tension, but it just fell into place; like Lego pieces, they just took one out and replaced it with another one. They all seem to date in the same circles.

"I think I'm the only one who has a real and true boyfriend. Ryan and I have been together since grade school, the cheer girl and the basketball star. We're deeply in love and getting married after high school. Here's my promise ring." She smiles contently and points to her left hand, where she wears a silver band with a rose-pink heart-shaped stone in it.

"It's very pretty. That's really special that you found someone you want to marry already. This dating thing is new to me, but I do like Taylor so far," I say.

"You and Taylor got along well last night. I asked Ryan to bring Taylor for you. He's sweet and nice looking too. He's not in sports, but he's really smart and a musician, so I thought he'd be perfect for you," she giggles.

"Oh, I'm not smart," I laugh. "I'm just an average student. People often think if you're good at art, you're intellectual. It's a completely different part of the brain."

"Well, it's smart that you know about the brain. I barely make it through school. I want to get good grades, but other things get in the way. I have to work out all the new routines and teach them to Rachel and Amanda, so we can all teach them to the girls. It's exhausting," she confesses.

"You're so talented, you could be a dancer. But I did notice you're the one behind the poms' success," I say.

"I don't know about that, but I'm happy to stay in the background. The power struggle in the group gets a little crazy. When Rachel was voted captain of the poms team, Amanda went ballistic. She feels she's the rightful heir to that throne. In fact, I'm shocked she's taking the homecoming queen defeat so well. Wait for the fallout on that one. Anyway, she hand-selected all of us to be an elite group of the prettiest and most talented in poms. I think she picked me because I'm the one who comes up with all the dance routines. She makes me teach them to her first and then tells Rachel we both came up with them. I don't care. There are many benefits to being among the most popular kids in school, so it's a small price to pay. I mean, how many poor kids like us get to go to each dance in a super stretch limo and spend the night in a mansion?"

Popularity

I smile, daydreaming for a moment. Now that I'm in the popular group, I'm looking forward to it. It's so new, I still pinch myself to make sure it's real.

"But it is a lot of work. Besides poms practice and the routine, I need to create and sew new outfits all the time to keep up with the designer stuff the other girls just buy," Ashley remarks.

"Whatever you're doing, it's working. Your clothes are so stylish. I would never guess that you don't buy off the rack like the other girls," I say.

"Thanks for keeping my secret. I know I can trust you. It's nice to have someone to talk about this stuff with. You'll find out, in the squad, there's no room for doubts, feelings or complaints; everything is scripted to suit the narrative. To the outside world, the beautiful popular people have no problems. Life is perfect. You'll see—maintaining that persona is a lot of work."

I'm grateful to have her as my guide through the world of popularity. And I hear what she says, but it doesn't faze me. Anything worthwhile takes hard work, my mom says. I see her work night and day at her jobs to give me a good life and I see Ev's moms do the same for all their kids. I can get up a little earlier and pay more attention to my appearance if it means I get to hold my head up high and walk with the most beautiful and popular girls in school. Plus, there's the parties, the dances, the boys. It's a dream come true.

When Ashley drops me off, I find my mom waiting for me in the house. She's dying to know how it all went. I tell her everything in detail from the dance to the party afterward and brunch this morning. We have that kind of relationship. It's been just the two of us for so long, we're like best friends.

"I like Taylor, Mom. And I really like kissing too. It's a little weird at first, but if you get that warm tingling feeling every time, I want to do it more." I grin with enthusiasm.

"I don't know if kissing is always that nice, but your first is special. It sounds like you had a wonderful time. I can only imagine what it's like inside that house," my mom says.

I also told her what happened to Ev at the dance. I don't want too much time to go by before I talk to her. It hurts. She lashed out like it's my fault. But after what happened to her, I don't blame her much. Still, I think we need to talk it out, so I ride my bike to her house.

Popularity

It's a typical day at her busy house with all the kids playing in the yard and toys and games strewn over the lawn. Sometimes her house looks like a circus or a daycare, but it's such a loving fun place to be, it makes the chaos worthwhile.

I leave my bike and walk down the drive toward her slowly and carefully, as I don't know how I'll be received.

"You don't have to tiptoe. It's fine." Ev laughs and waves for me to join her.

It is a hot day, so she's spraying some kids with the hose as they run by her, screaming in delight.

"You don't want to spray me in vengeance," I laugh, holding my hands in the air.

"Nah. I was upset last night. I'm sorry I yelled at you," she says and shoots me half a smile.

"That's ok. Did you get the suit clean?" I ask.

"Yeah, my mom's a wizard at getting stains out. With this brood you have to be. We need to reuse clothes a lot," she says.

"By the way, you looked really pretty last night."

Since we seem mended, I tell her about the afterparty and kissing Taylor.

"Well, I don't know much about kissing boys, but I guess kissing is the same with girls too. When I kiss Elli, she always has a different flavor gloss on her lips. It's kind of fun not knowing whether it's going to be bubble gum, cherry, or peach flavor," she says.

"I guess that's different; boys don't have flavored lips... at least I think they don't," I say and we both laugh as she squirts a little bit of water at me.

We play with her brothers and sisters in the water for a while and then dry off and eat Popsicles on her front porch with the kids.

"To be honest, I feel threatened by your new friends. I don't want to lose you," she admits.

"No way," I laugh and loop my arm around hers. "We're best friends forever. Nothing will change that. This is just something I've always wanted to do. I'm not like you. You're confident in who you are. I don't know who I am, but I like who I am when I'm with them."

"Just be careful," she says. "Plastic melts into something unrecognizable when under intense heat."

I stay for a while longer, but as this is my mom's one day off, I want to spend some time with her too.

When I get home, my mom and I have a nice dinner on our back porch. We have a campfire pit and love to sit around and watch it glow.

"I read something online about an art contest. I thought you might be interested," she says and hands me some papers. "The first prize can put you in the running for scholarships to art school. I know it's a few years away, but you never know."

The printout says there's a theme and you need to create original artwork about being a teen.

Ideas immediately whirl around in my head. What is being a teen? How do you draw that?

It's an intriguing idea, and any scholarship money would take some of the burden off my mom. She believes in my art and wants to send me to a good art school, but those don't come cheap. She squirrels away everything to help, but I realize I may need to work for a few years myself to make it happen.

I go to bed and scroll through my Instagram and TikTok feeds. I don't want to always be the lost little mascot lamb in The Glam Squad, so I need to do some research to keep improving myself.

Finding a few new makeup, hair and clothes accounts, I make a short list of ideas, from flat irons to tame my frizzy mane to flavored lip gloss. I like the idea of keeping Taylor on his toes with unique tastes of cherry, grape or bubble gum with each kiss. I can pick some up after school at the dollar store or discount store along with the flat iron and some other supplies. It'll cut into my art budget, but maybe I can pick up some more hours at my mom's work to cover it.

The next day, I wake up an hour early so I can get ready for school. I need to wash and properly dry my hair so it doesn't frizz. I have some of the products the girls told me about, so I add them in after shampooing and carefully use a brush to control the curl while drying on a low heat.

It's a lot of work and takes a long time. My hair is shoulder length, but to dry each curl with a brush on the low heat is tedious. I almost give up and nearly miss the bus, but it's worth it. My hair actually looks nice. I pull it into a side ponytail and wrap a ribbon around it. And, of course, I use gel to keep it in place, but for the first time, I start to see a Glam Girl looking back at me in the mirror.

When I get on the bus, I can tell people are eyeing me, and maybe even admiring me. I like it.

And at school, I experience the same thing. If I knew all I had to do was primp a lot to get attention, I would've done it a long time ago.

The big test, though, is walking with the glam girls down the hall. Instead of their geeky artist sidekick, I'm a real member of the squad now. I join them at the end of the hallway. As we walk, people look at us. I try to use only my peripheral vision, but I hold my head up a little higher and start to strut tall and proud, like a runway model.

It's so fun to be noticed. It's exhilarating. And in class, boys and girls call me by my name for the first time. Some girls even compliment my hair and outfit.

Now in class, I'm not slumping down as low as possible in my former effort to seem invisible.

Lunch is my favorite time. We glide into the outdoor cafeteria area with our little purses for lunch. Glam girls don't use trays—they're bulky, and besides, these girls don't eat a lot. Some fruit, carrots or celery with water or a diet soda, a bag of pretzels or some French fries are the norm. You can have a small petite sandwich or salad, no dressing. Nothing messy and everything must be contained in a small purse and eaten with small nibbles.

I sit with the girls, eating as daintily as possible, as they chatter about the dance, scroll through their phones and gossip about what people are wearing and who they're with.

"Oh, here's a meme of that unfortunate situation at the dance," Chloe says in an unemotional matter-of-fact tone.

"Here's another one. Yikes, that's not a good look," Alyssa says.

"I think it's trending—#christeningthequeen," Brittany adds.

I immediately pick up my phone to scroll through some of the more popular student posts for our school and see what's trending.

There are some videos and pictures on IG of the football players dousing Ev, but the worst part is the memes, mostly shared by the football guys.

One shows a picture of her soaked at the dance and says "maybe this will cleanse her evil ways." Another has Ev's head on a girl in a wet white T-shirt so can see through it. It says "just add water and make a girl from a toad."

The posts are all over social media and each one is worse than the last. I feel sick to my stomach. The other girls aren't laughing or anything, but they're not dismissing it either.

I look over at Ev in her group. She doesn't usually pay attention to social media, but I don't know if she can ignore this. It's like a hurricane of hate, all directed her way. I nearly get up to show her, but I figure it's best to tell her in private.

Amanda arrives late to lunch, making her typical entrance, and shows us her new video.

"I want you to be the first to preview my new video. I call it *Hail to the Queen*. It goes live tomorrow," she says proudly.

The video is to the song about being a rich girl and it shows video clips of her in places like her pool, on the beach and driving her car, in glamourous gowns and bikinis, and juxtaposes it with pictures of Rachel in very unflattering positions looking surprised, including some without makeup and one that was obviously taken in the locker room when she was getting changed. You don't see anything, though, because she's covered with a towel.

Then at the end of the video, Amanda is dressed in a queen's robe and small white balls of light fall, showering her in brilliant white radiance with an enormous shimmering crown on her head and a sparkler display that erupts in the words "The Real Queen."

We all look at each other in astonished quiet, not knowing what to say. It's mean to Rachel. I want to speak up, but since no one else is, I'm afraid to.

"This will show everyone who the real queen is." Amanda laughs with a bit of an evil chuckle.

Suddenly, I hear the sound of screams and crashes and turn my head around.

I'm not sure what starts it, but when I turn around I see Ev and her group and the football players face-to-face at Ev's table and the next thing I know, food is flying in the air, trays and chairs crash on the ground, and whistles blow amid yelling and shrieking.

The glam girls all move with the rest of the crowd toward the disruption, but I find myself paralyzed. Do I take Ev's side? What if she yells at me again? I want to melt into a pool of water and seep into the ground.

Teachers quickly intervene to break it up, but I don't want anyone to see me cower, so I run into the school building, hoping no one notices me. If I can pretend I don't see anything, I can't be blamed for taking sides. See no evil. Hear no evil.

Chapter Eleven
Cyberbullying

I hear through the grapevine that Ev went to the dean's office, so I go by her house later that day to see how it went. I want her to tell me and figure I'll pretend I don't know about what happened. I know it's wrong to lie to a friend, but it's survival mode now. I want to keep my new friends and Ev too.

I knock on the door and she answers with a casual smile on her face, like nothing was wrong.

"Just making sure you're ok. I hear you got called into the admin office," I say innocently.

"Ah, it's nothing. The dean's cool. There was a standoff at lunch with the football players, when they made some trouble. But I didn't get anything. She says she understands bullying, as she experienced it as a kid too. She gave it to the football players, though. She's making them sit out for Friday's big game to teach them a lesson," Ev explains.

My eyes grow into big circles when she tells me.

"Wow, this week's game is a conference championship.," I say, shocked.

"Of course you and your twaddle friends would know that," she snidely remarks.

"No, I'm just surprised. I'm glad you didn't get in trouble, but I'm afraid they'll get you back. Maybe just stay away from them. They have it out for you," I warn.

I show her the memes and videos on Instagram. She looks at them and just laughs.

"I don't care. I'm not afraid of them. This is their hang up, not mind," Ev insists with indifference and suggests we play a game.

As I follow her into their living room, I'm not so sure it'll be that easy. If the team loses, they may turn the entire school against her. I hope not.

After a few hours, I ride home, pick out and prepare tomorrow's outfit and slip into bed, but not before checking my social media.

Popularity

I can't shake the feeling that the football players will go after Ev, but then I get notifications that Amanda posted a video on YouTube, Instagram and TikTok. It's the one she showed us the day before.

It already has over 2,000 likes and a bunch of comments. There are only 1,000 kids in our school, but with Amanda's following, it could go viral quickly.

I scroll through the comments, and some are really nasty. They range from calling Rachel names to talking about her body. I read a few and shut my phone off. This is bad. I feel sorry for Rachel. She's nice and doesn't deserve it. I know why Amanda did it and none of us agreed, but we didn't say anything either. I should have said something. Now it's too late.

I'm going to say something to Amanda, anyway. Maybe she can take it down and limit the damage. I know how heartbreaking and degrading it is to be teased and bullied, and it's not right. I'm not sure how to say it, but I should say something.

The next day, it gets worse. Within five minutes of walking through the school doors, I hear the chatter spread like a virus. In the halls, everyone's checking their phones. A boy in school took a screenshot of Amanda's video where she shows Rachel with the towel, but someone changed the screenshot and posted the altered photo on Snapchat as a topless picture with the line "If you want to see more, call..." but he actually put her phone number on the post. And it has 5,000 likes and counting.

By lunch, everybody's seen the post. I hear a lot of boys and girls laughing at it—to be honest, mostly boys. Many girls are upset. It's obviously not her body. He photoshopped it, but the horrid comment train is running off the rails with out-of-control remarks piling up on the poor girl.

At The Glam Squad lunch table, Brittany brings it up first.

"I can't believe that picture of Rachel. It's awful. It doesn't even look like her," she says.

"Brittany! It's not her. But that's not even the point. No one has the right to post someone's phone number online or post pictures of them like that," Ashley says in angered indignation.

"Well, I think we need to find out whoever did it and take him out," Chloe says with an outraged fervor.

"Oh, it'll pass. Snapchat is only for one day. And she can always change her phone number," Alyssa says.

"I feel sorry for her," I add. "It's no fun being bullied."

The minute the words leave my lips, I hear gasps coming at me like tires leaking air.

"Bullying?" Brittany and Alyssa say in disbelief.

"That's not bullying. It's a stupid trick, but it's not like someone hit her or pushed her," Brittany says.

"Are you serious, Brittany? You don't have to physically assault someone to bully them—right, Mel?" Ashley says with confidence.

"Emotional scars often hurt as much as a black eye and last longer. It's very difficult to come back from," I say softly with my head down.

"I guess so. I never thought of that," Brittany says curiously.

I shouldn't be surprised that I'm the token misfit in the group who must explain to the beautiful people what it's like to be bullied. Since they are members of the popular club, I guess none of them could ever understand being teased. But then again, popularity and beauty didn't protect Rachel from harm. Maybe anyone can be a target.

Strangely, Amanda never shows up for lunch, and the other girls mention they didn't see her in classes. I wonder if maybe she regrets that her video started the whole campaign against Rachel and she's skipping until it all dies down.

When I get to poms practice after school, there's a hushed huddle of girls sitting on the field talking.

"Rachel's gutted—she's not coming to practice today," one girl says.

"I don't know if I'd ever come back," another adds.

"Is it that bad?" Alyssa asks.

"Yes, Alyssa, she's been getting awful text messages all day. Guys are texting her naked pictures of themselves, calling her terrible names and making vile suggestions. Her parents talked to the dean. She may change schools," barks Caroline, Rachel's best friend.

"Sorry, I just asked," Alyssa says sarcastically, but quietly.

"Wow, I didn't know it is such a big deal," Brittany says somberly.

Popularity

"It is a big deal, Brittany. I just don't understand why people think they have the right to do that," Caroline says angrily.

"Nobody's saying it, but Amanda's video started it all," another girl says.

"No, no, Amanda's video isn't very nice, but she never intended for this to happen," Alyssa defends.

"She just wanted to get back at Rachel for stealing her crown," Brittany adds, defending Amanda.

"Stealing her crown? Amanda lost. If her fragile baby ego can't handle that, she has real problems!" Caroline shouts back.

"Now, just a minute. Amanda's not here to stand up for herself," Chloe chimes in.

"I did notice that she's not here. Is she too cowardly to face us?" Caroline says.

One girl stands up and points a finger at Chloe. "You Glam Squad girls will support your leader no matter what. She started it all. It's her fault!" she accuses.

Then Chloe jumps up and gets face to face with the girl. "I just think Amanda has a right to stick up for herself without people slurring her name and our group," she fires back.

The girl pushes Chloe, who pushes her back. Everything gets intense, with some girls shouting at each other and a couple poking and pushing one another, until the coach blows her whistle loudly.

"We're a team here, ladies. Let's act like one. We're at least one girl down at this point and we need to pull together to cover the gaps. Don't forget we have a game tomorrow," the coach commands.

They start practicing, but the tension is clearly interfering with their usually tight dance formations.

My mind drifts to Amanda. What is she thinking? Why isn't she here? Or at school?

She didn't expect what happened, but she did want her video to ridicule Rachel as a means of revenge.

I text her to check on her.

"Ok?" I write.

I don't get a response.

As I get into bed a few hours later, I hear a chime on my phone. It's Amanda.

"All good." she replies.

I don't know what she means, but I'm relieved she's ok. I don't agree with what she did, but she's my friend.

Popularity

The next day is the conference championship, and the school gossip mill is buzzing about the standoff between the dean and the football coach.

Kids who work in the admin office overhear and the text chain quickly bubbles up like a witch's brew with smoke oozing out of a cauldron.

"She called him a neanderthal," one text says.

"He says she's out to get the football program so he'll retire," another text claims.

"The coach threatened the dean and she gave it right back to him and fired him," another text stream alleges.

It's a molten hot scandal and no one knows what's true. The whole school's talking about it and texting everyone they know.

The texts say the dean and the coach had a tangle in her office about her suspension of the five players for their actions at the dance and subsequent fight with Ev at school, as it violated the school's zero tolerance bullying policy.

The coach is obviously upset, as several of the five are starting players, including their star kicker.

The entire day is strained as everyone anticipates the game ahead. You could literally cut the tension with a knife.

I'm looking forward to chem class to get away from the gossip. Ev and I are partners and she never reads the texts, so I can get a break. But when I get to our table, I see someone wrote "Dyke" and "Butch" on our table.

I try to wipe it off before Ev comes in, but it's in permanent marker. When she sees it, she just laughs.

"I do think I have a unique style, but it's not wrong. I am what I am."

She's not upset, but I am. The past week has me reeling with how hurtful people can be. I spent my childhood being the subject of teasing, snickers and name-calling for being weird, since I was a shy wallflower. That's tough and it made me revere and envy the popular kids for being untouchable. But with what happened to Rachel, it seems like anyone is fair game. And I worry about Ev. I have a bad feeling about where this is going.

Popularity

The game is packed. It's understandable that a championship game would be crowded, but it looks like the entire school is here to see what happens.

Ev comes too. She didn't listen when I told her to stay home. She says she's not going to let those jerks dictate her behavior, but I think even the strongest warrior can be vulnerable. At least she sits in the student bleacher section with Elli this time to stay out of the football player's sight.

Then Amanda shows up in uniform and turns my attention to the poms team. She wasn't at school for two days, but since Rachel isn't dancing, they need another person for the routine, so the poms coach lets Amanda perform even though she wasn't at school that day.

I'm on the edge of my seat waiting for the explosion to continue from yesterday's practice. Caroline and her group sit in silence around one bench while The Glam Squad, including me, sit on the adjacent bench. No one looks at each other and no one talks to each other.

The football game isn't as bad as people predicted. Many of the banned players are linemen, who were replaced. The kicker and the running back are the big holes in the lineup. And the coach is here, so that blows up the rumors of his dismissal.

Coach has a grisly look on his face at the beginning of the game, but the quarterback and the other players fill in the gaps and switch to a running game. By halftime, the score is 14 to 10 in favor of our team. The crowd is hopeful and I'm relieved.

But now it's halftime and time for the poms to perform.

Given the silent standoff in the different factions of the poms team, I'm not sure how they'll perform. It's stiff at first, but everyone does their job and goes back to their respective benches without a word. The usual joy and exuberance in their dancing are definitely missing. It's like robots going through the motions.

And I detect the animosity between Caroline and Amanda. Most people wouldn't notice it, but I've seen their routines so many times. I see Caroline deliberately put her poms in Amanda's face and cut her off a couple times. It's subtle and doesn't cause a break in the choreography, but Amanda knows what happened. I'm not sure how that'll go down.

After the poms perform, the band does a quick show and the announcer goes through some sponsors. Given the affluence of the school, they have a big video screen on the scoreboard to show different angles on the field, mostly during the halftime performances or special events and they often show commercials for sponsors.

No one pays much attention to the commercials, but suddenly we hear music and a video pops up on the scoreboard screen.

It is a video of Ev and Elli kissing at the dance and it is playing the song about kissing the girl and liking it.

I hold my breath and look around frantically for Ev. People are laughing and pointing. Then on the screen it says "Evelyn Glen-Marks is a gay dirty dyke." And it shows the picture of her soaked at the dance.

I nearly wrench my neck trying to find Ev and spot her running down the bleacher stairs after Elli, who's sobbing and running away.

The screen switches to a feed of Ev's house with toilet paper all over the trees and lawn. And written in red paint on their house is the word "GAY."

When that comes up, Ev stops and everyone's stunned into silence. It's way over the line. Maybe they are just targeting her and not her moms too, but they clearly showed her address on purpose and vandalized her home. That's just plain cruel.

I start to cry and run after Ev.

It takes only minutes for the video to pop up all over social media, only hours for it to go viral, and even less time for the memes to begin circulating via text, posts, and shared posts. In no time, the video is in the hands of every student in school.

It's insane how fast and deep the cuts go on social media and text. I admit, I usually like the fun videos and memes, but when it's used for the wrong reasons, it critically wounds people. Plus, it's not just the kids in school; it's adults too. On the internet, it spreads wide. It's really unfair.

That video cracked Ev. I catch up to Ev in the parking lot. She calls her mom to pick her up. She's mad and stewing in silence, looking straight ahead and breathing heavily. I can see she doesn't want to talk, so I hold her hand and wait with her.

I go home with them and stay overnight at Ev's. The toilet paper is all over their front yard and the gay slurs are in two places on the house. She sees it, but just stares ahead and doesn't say anything. She's still seething and doesn't talk much all night. We watch a scary movie in silence to take our minds off the game and try to fall asleep.

Popularity

In the morning, we work on cleanup, but Ev hasn't changed her expression. It's blank like a stone. I don't think the video of her and the name-calling dented her armor, but when they included her family, that was it. She's not talking, just empty. I've never seen her this way.

The cleanup takes all weekend, but we all know the harassment will continue. Ev's moms keep the younger kids in the house. They know what comes next.

As we wash the paint off the house and pick up the toilet paper, cars go by honking and yelling mean and disgusting slurs out the window to us. I feel horrible. It's humiliating and wrong. Ev's family didn't hurt anyone and I can tell it has the whole house upset.

When I go inside to get a drink, I overhear Ev's moms talking. Janis is furious, but Lucy calms her down. It's clear they don't care about themselves, but they worry about how the hatred and bullying is affecting Ev and the other kids.

"Something has to be done!" Janis roars.

"You know how this goes—we fight and it gets worse. Better to let it pass and people will forget and move onto something else," Lucy reasons.

"I want to talk to the school. I don't like what it's doing to Evelyn. She's hurting. Should we take her out of school? Should we move?" Janis asks.

"She's going to have to deal with these narrow-minded bigots her whole life, just like we do. It's a hard lesson. Let's just take a breath and see what tomorrow looks like," Lucy says.

I forget about the drink and walk out the door. I'm not thirsty anymore. I make an excuse to Ev that my mom texted and wants me home and ride home in tears. I don't want Ev to leave.

Chapter Twelve
New Life

I go to school on Monday, still destroyed at the thought of losing my best friend. I'm sad and furious at those stupid bullies.

The minute I walk into school, I feel like I entered a whirlwind. Every hour seems to bring a new development in the wake of what happened at Friday's game.

The dean was at the game and viewed the video online too. It's deleted by Monday morning, but she has the police trace it back to the IP address and knows it's one of the suspended football players, so one or all of them could have been involved.

The gossip mill quotes a reliable source in the admin office that the dean called them into her office one at a time and forced some confessions. It turns out three of the five players had the video put up and vandalized Ev's house.

I also hear she suspended them from school for one month and removed them from the football team permanently. They won't be playing in the regional championship game—or any—game anymore.

And people saw the coach an hour later barreling into the dean's office with a red face and full head of steam. Their screaming match could be heard by everyone in the crowd gathered outside the admin office to listen in.

It ends with the coach storming out. Later, we find out she fired him. That shocks everyone in school, since the team is right in the middle of a huge season.

After school and before poms practice, I watch the football players in the adjacent field. They look lost and so does the assistant coach who now has to fill in. I feel terrible for the remaining players. Some of these guys need big wins to earn scholarships. If they come from my side of town, they need the money to go to college.

And even the rich kids are affected. I never thought about it much, but some of them get a lot of pressure from their family to excel in sports. It's a trophy for their connected parents to boast about their successful athletic child to their friends and associates. It's messed up, but true.

Popularity

The next day at lunch, Chloe told me she heard some of the dads are going to try to get the dean removed by the school board.

I don't know what's going to happen. The rich parents carry a lot of weight at the school. The dean did the right thing, but now so many lives are falling like dominos, as my mom says. It's so stupid. All of this is because some people don't like that Ev dates girls and that she ran for homecoming queen.

I keep coming back to the same thing. Why do they care if Ev or anyone else likes boys or girls? No one cares who I date. What's the difference? It doesn't make any sense.

These days, I can barely catch my breath before something else happens. It's like a roller coaster.

After school, as the poms girls start to show up for practice, I'm afraid of another big blowup, but in a big surprise, Amanda diffuses the entire thing.

"I just want everyone to know that I regret what happened to Rachel. The video was petty revenge on my part, but I really didn't expect the rest to happen. I guess I underestimated the stupidity and brutality of other people. But I started it and I take full responsibility for my part. I took the video down immediately when I heard about the texted picture and have sent Rachel an apology. I won't blame her if she doesn't accept. And I don't fault any of you who hold me liable for the damage. I'll resign from the team if you want me to," she states with a solemn voice.

My jaw is on the ground. I didn't expect that from Amanda. Watching her, I believe she really means what she said. Maybe she sees how destructive revenge can be.

It did the trick. I see the coldness of the team strife melt right before my eyes. The practice goes well, and the team is back to normal, except Rachel. I don't know if she's coming back.

Everyone goes to Stars after practice, with Amanda treating. After the last week, it's the break we all need. The music booms, the burgers, fries and shakes are plentiful. The girls on the poms team seem to be moving on. I'm glad. The last week has been exhausting.

Ashley offers to take me home after we're done and we glide along in her pink Bug with the warm breeze lifting my hair all over. It'll be a mess when I get home, but it's refreshing. With the wind flowing over me, I almost let the tension go and relax a bit.

"You know she doesn't mean a word of it, don't you?" Ashley says.

"Who?"

"Amanda. That speech is so phony. Rachel's not around, Amanda's forgiven and I'm sure she'll slip into the captain's spot. She got everything she wanted."

Ashley's voice has a lot of sarcasm in it. I don't understand why she thinks that, and I don't agree. Amanda seemed genuinely sorry, but I just let it wash over me. We had a good time at Stars. I want to move forward.

A few weeks later, everything calms down. Especially after the football team won regionals without the coach, the school is looking ahead to victory and all else is yesterday's news.

The school atmosphere is exciting and I'm enjoying my new life. No longer am I wallpaper—I'm on the stage.

It's a whole new world. Each day, I comb TikTok and Instagram to look at new hair, makeup and clothing styles.

To be honest, it's like another class to study for, but I love it.

One of my new tools is a flat iron to tame and straighten my curly mane. It's taken some trial and error, along with a little singed hair, but I'm finally getting the hang of it.

I can pull the sleek hair back into a ponytail or let it hang, either with or without a clip. I love it. I feel sophisticated.

My dating life is improving too. Since the dance, Taylor and I have been going out with Ryan and Ashley. We've become a very comfortable famous foursome, going to the movies, playing miniature golf, and heading out for tacos, burgers and pizza together. It's a great way to get to know Taylor without so much pressure. I like to kiss and hold hands, but that's all I'm ready for.

I like dating Taylor. I never realized what I was missing. He walks me to class and I have someone to go everywhere with. And he texts me funny memes and pictures. He's hilarious.

I really think he likes me, at least I hope so. I like him.

And hanging out with Ashley and Ryan has made wading into the dating pool much easier. She and Ryan have

Popularity

been together for so long; they're the template for a good relationship.

She's a good friend. We take trips to the dollar store and Goodwill to find potential outfits and discount makeup, material and other beautifications. She's on a budget too and knows a lot of tricks.

She's so creative. She makes something that costs a nickel look like it costs a dollar. I'm getting better, but I'm not at her level. My nickel outfits look like they cost a dime—maybe a quarter. I'm still learning. . .

And since she has a car, we go to the stores in the next town so we don't run into anyone we know. Her secret is my sacred vow.

Anytime we're together, she talks a lot about her wedding. I don't mind. It's fun and sweet to see a girl just a little older than me so sure about her path in life.

I'm not in that place at all, but I've been let into her bubble. I think we've developed a kinship of sorts. She shows me her storyboards for the planning and confides in me about the costs of the wedding and her insecurities. I'm the only one she can tell.

We're at my house, poring over bridal sites and magazines and she gives me the complete picture of the wedding. It's like I can see it.

"I'm doing an Old Hollywood theme with a lot of glitz, glamor and glitter. Of course, I'm making my gown and everyone will dress in the style. Here's my idea for the tables. I'm going to get some inexpensive picture frames and paint and 'Ashify' them with glitter and sequins and devote each to a famous Old Hollywood couple. And I found these cheaper tall slim plastic vases so they hold fewer flowers and maybe some feathers. I'll drape them in fabric and apply sequins to make each look rich. But Ryan's family is well off and I don't know what they'll make of my homemade craft projects."

"I think your theme will be so beautiful and stylish. No one will pay attention if there's crystal on the tables. I could draw some giant silhouettes of different glam couples and you could use them, if you want," I offer.

She screams in delight and jumps up and hugs me. I'm happy to help, to pay back all her kindness and friendship.

Like she says, we poor girls have to stick together. We even have our own secret code. When the other girls

Popularity

talk about all their designer clothes and the things they buy, we make our eyes wide and blink at each other three times. It's a blast.

Glamor is expensive, and with dating and so many friend obligations, I've had to cut down on work and art. But it's worth it. I still work a few hours on Saturdays and Sundays during the day. But I pretty much cut out babysitting. I need date nights free now.

I've had to sacrifice some things. Art will always be there. I want to live in the here and now. I love it.

But I'm sad that Ev has been distant. I think she still links my new friends with those dumb football players who bullied her. Maybe it's my fault. I try to spend time with her, but it's hard. I want to tell her about everything going on in my life, but she hates The Glam Squad and when I talk about Taylor, she gets uneasy and quickly changes the subject.

Brittany and Alyssa say Ev *like* likes me, but they're wrong. We've been friends for a long time, since before she told me she's gay.

It's a shame I have to keep my lives and friends separate, but I don't want to lose Ev as a friend, so I invite her over for a popcorn and movie night one Sunday. Since it's a school night, we have to get special permission from our moms.

We're streaming a superhero movie and eating pizza. It's like old times, except my phone keeps blowing up. I put it on silent, but the screen lights up when I get a notification and it distracts me.

Ashley texts me a wedding inspiration pic and Taylor sends me a funny meme. Brittany texts some gossip and I get a notification that Amanda posted a new video. I try not to look at it, but I find myself glancing once in a while. I can't help it—I'm curious—but Ev notices right away.

"Are you serious with that phone? Why don't you have it implanted into your brain so all your secret little twaddle messages get to you faster?" she says sarcastically.

"I'm sorry, they're online a lot," I apologize. I shove my phone under a couch pillow.

Then she turns the TV off and grabs her backpack.

"No. If that nonsense means so much to you, I don't want to take you away from it. Go ahead. I'm out."

She stomps toward the door with a head of steam and I follow her.

"You don't have to go," I say.

"Yes, I do. You're not the same person as you used to be. You're not around and even when you are, you're not here!" Ev shouts.

I can hear the pain and anger in her voice, but nothing I say can make a difference. Then I get defensive.

"You're not the same either. Why can't you accept my new life? And anytime I mention Taylor, you change the subject. I listen to you talk about your girlfriends!" I yell back.

"Oooo, Taylor," she says in a high-pitched voice and makes a weird scrunched face like she smells something rancid.

I can't help myself. All my emotions boil to the surface. I'm mad at her for being distant. I'm angry that she makes fun of everything that's important to me. And when I try to spend time with her, she acts this way. I lose it.

"Maybe the girls are right. Maybe you are jealous of Taylor."

The second the words leave my mouth, I regret it. I didn't mean it.

She's really quiet and stares at me with a dire sadness in her eyes. It's like she's looking through me.

"I really hope you don't think that," she says somberly and looks down.

"You're straight, I'm not. It doesn't mean I want you as a girlfriend. That's not the way we do things. But I thought we could always be friends. I guess not."

She walks out the door and doesn't look back.

After she leaves, I start crying and continue all night, while shoveling the rest of the pizza and popcorn in my mouth, along with a bunch of mini chocolate bars. I didn't mean to hurt her, but I ended up hurting us both.

For a week, I text and send her apology memes and emojis, but no response. I'm not going to say it's over. She'll come around. I just need to give her some time and space.

Chapter Thirteen
The Accident

The football team's sectional championship is about 30 miles away in a nearby town. Everyone in school is buzzing about it. There are posters all over the hallways and we had a pep rally where the poms performed.

It's the first time our football team has gotten this far. If the team wins, they get to compete in the semifinals for the state championship. They've never won state. It's a big deal.

Since the game is at another school, our band and poms won't be performing, but we all still want to go. The poms think they can start something in the stands to pep up school spirit for the team.

The school is sending buses with anyone who wants to go, but Amanda borrows her father's SUV so we can all ride together. The girls are going to wear their poms outfits and cheer from the visitors' bleachers.

Even if the team wins, the state championships are far away. This may be the only chance we have to show our school spirit and support the team, so it seems like the whole school is going. It's the event of the year.

I need to ask my mom if I can go with Amanda. She let me stay at Amanda's house after the dance, so I don't think it'll be a big deal.

But for two nights in a row my mom gets stuck at work and doesn't come home until I'm asleep. She works really hard for us.

She'll be home before I have to leave and I know she'll say yes, so I start planning my outfit for the night's game. I don't have a poms uniform, but I'm going to be sitting with them, so I put together a long shirt and pants, all in school colors, and an iron on a drawing I made of our school logo, similar to the poms uniforms. And I style my hair the same way, so I will blend in with them. I'm almost an official member of the team anyway; I go to all their practices.

I can't wait to show my mom the outfit I made for the big game. I don't care about football much, but it's hard not to get caught up in all the hoopla over sectionals.

But when she gets home, she's mad.

"Did you completely cut your work hours this weekend?" She sounds more like she's accusing me than asking.

"Yes, since you've been working late, I didn't have the chance to tell you, but I'm going to the big game with the girls tonight and Amanda's invited everyone to stay at her house after. She's making a whole big weekend of it. It'll be so much fun," I say.

She looks down and shakes her head.

"And have you mailed your submission for the school art contest yet?"

"I have a week. I've just been really busy with the girls and Taylor and work and all," I explain.

She sighs and slams her bag down in frustration.

"I'm getting concerned that you're spending so much time with these new friends—you're neglecting other things like your art and work. Plus, you're investing a lot of your money in your new look," she says, calming down.

"I'm just changing things some. I can juggle a lot of balls at the same time. Don't worry," I tell her.

"I am worried. I'm not sure I like the influence of these people and all their money. It doesn't seem like you. Maybe you shouldn't go over there for another weekend."

"Not go? I have to go! I need to go. First Ev, now you—I don't understand why people are against me improving," I say angrily.

"For the first time in my life, I'm somebody. People look at me like I'm important. They envy me. Do you know what it's like for someone like me to be cast from the shadows into the spotlight? I'm seen for the first time in my life. I like it and I'm not giving it up!"

Then I hear Amanda beeping outside, and I pick up my bag and storm out of the house, nearly in tears. As I walk to the car, I collect myself and paste on a smile. I don't want the girls to see me upset. I love my mom, but she doesn't understand what it's like to be me.

Amanda's driving, Chloe is in the front seat, and Ashley, Brittany and I are in the back. I volunteer to take the middle. It's a big car, so there's plenty of room. Alyssa had to be there early for something, so she drove with her dance date, Astin, who's on the team.

Popularity

I'm surprised at the luxury of the SUV. I've never been in such a fancy car, even the dance limo. The exterior is a gold metallic, so it sparkles and gleams in the setting sun. And the seats are so soft and smooth to the touch, they feel like an expensive suede coat. And there are white LED lights running on the ceiling and the doors.

It's drive time and there's a lot of traffic, but we're having a good time. The music is booming and, as usual, everyone's talking at the same time while showing each other things on their phones.

Before we know it, 20 minutes go by and we're stuck in gridlock.

Amanda's phone is blowing up as other poms girls are wondering where she is. They had a whole routine planned for before the game started and we're running very late.

She's getting frustrated and asking the car's navigation for detours around the traffic. Each time the voice proposes a new direction and ETA, we learn the route will still take too long.

Amanda roars at the bodyless voice until it shows a path that will take 15 minutes.

"There! If we take this one, we'll make it for the beginning of the game," she says.

"If we don't, the girls can do it without us. You can't make the traffic disappear," Chloe says.

"No! No one is doing my routine without me. I'm the leader!" she howls at Chloe, like a demon with red glowing eyes.

We're all a little stunned at her reaction. After the Rachel incident, she's biding her time in the poms' good graces, trying to be named captain. But it's still a delicate situation.

Amanda veers onto an offramp and turns onto another route. Instead of the highway, now we're driving through small suburban towns and then in a more rural area with fewer crossroads.

"Good, the speed limit is 65 here." Amanda smiles and accelerates.

Time's ticking away and Amanda's phone is binging and bonging regularly. She seems desperate to get there on time and more agitated with each notification. But we all ignore it.

Popularity

Ashley is resting her head against the window. Earlier she said she didn't feel well, but she really wanted to go to the game anyway.

I leave her alone and since Brittany's preoccupied with her phone, I look on mine to see a text from Taylor. He and Ashley's boyfriend, Ryan, are already at the game. He's sending me pictures of the stadium—the crowd is huge.

Everyone's looking at their phones as they get updates from people at the game, including Amanda. She's texting Caroline updates on our time of arrival. We're five minutes away.

I hear Chloe scream and we all look up. A pickup truck is coming right at us from the side.

Everything happens in a hazy slow motion. I'm pushed up against Brittany and my head is in her lap. I see Amanda fall forward into the steering wheel and Chloe hit her head on the dashboard as the airbags inflate with a whooshing sound.

The shrieks are muffled by the time lapse in my head. Every minute seems as if it takes 10 minutes. Phones and purses are floating around, almost suspended in midair, as we all are piled into the right half of the car as it tips over.

I feel as if I'm watching the whole thing occur from the outside looking in. It's not real.

Then there's silence. I hear nothing.

When I awake, everything is foggy, but the sounds are loud. It's dark and I'm lying down. People are shouting, earsplitting sirens are shrilling and everyone is moving at a sped-up pace, like when you fast forward through parts of a movie.

I must have blacked out again, because when I awake this time, I see a bright light. I'm in a room and a lady is next to me. I think it's my mom, but my eyes are still a little blurry.

She's holding my left hand. My right arm is heavy. I hold it up and stare at it as if it's foreign to me. It's in a blue cast and hard to raise.

"Mom?" I say in a confused groggy voice.

"It's all fine, honey. Don't worry. You're going to be just fine." She strokes my hair and puts her hand on my forehead.

Everything's scrambled in my brain. How did I get here? Why am I here? But I can only get a few words out.

"What happened?" I ask.

"You girls were in an accident. But you're fine. You just broke your arm and hand," she says. "Now, just lie still and rest. They have you on some pain medication, so it's ok to sleep."

I'm not able to focus my brain or my vision. I try to think of what I saw, the accident, but it's not clear and I fall back to sleep.

I wake again and look around the room. My vision is clearer and I feel more aware, but still confused.

"You're up—good. I wondered if you would sleep forever." My mom smiles at me and sticks a straw in my mouth.

"Here, have a sip of water; you've been out for nearly 20 hours, so you must be thirsty."

I drink some water.

"Mom, I don't understand what I'm doing here," I say.

She looks at me and sighs.

"You girls were in an accident. A truck hit the SUV from the side. You don't remember?" she says gently.

I rack my brain, but I just shake my head. I don't remember anything.

"Don't worry about it. You may remember later. Maybe it's better if you don't," she says.

My mind's all garbled. I remember driving in the SUV to the game, but then nothing.

"Where are the other girls? Are they ok?" I ask.

"Brittany has a broken leg and arm, Chloe broke her ankle and has some bumps and bruises and Amanda broke her ribs and has to have some glass removed from her face. She'll be fine, though," she says.

I shake my head again, trying to focus, but nothing comes. Then I remember Ashley was sitting next to me and I panic.

"What about Ashley?" I ask.

My mom puts her head down, and gazes straight at me and sadly nods her head back and forth.

"What does that mean?" I insist.

She grasps my hand and squeezes.

"I'm sorry, honey. Ashley didn't make it."

I try, but I don't understand. It just doesn't sink in.

Chapter Fourteen
The Aftermath

I spend the next day coming out of a fog. I still can't remember anything or register what happened to me, to us, to Ashley.

When Ev comes in toward the middle of the day, her face is wet and tears are streaming down from her eyes.

"I'm so happy to see you. When I heard you were in a car accident, I couldn't believe it. I thought I might lose you. It tore me up." She buries her head down on my bed, crying.

"I'm ok. Don't worry," I say with detachment, and I pat her blue hair.

She looks at me with that crinkled nose like I'm crazy.

"Are you sure you're ok? You sound strange," Ev says.

"Maybe I am. I don't know. My mom says I'm on medication. That could be it," I say in a daze.

My eyes are focused, but I can't retain much information or form any real thoughts. When I'm alone, I strain to comprehend the littlest things.

When I wake up the next day, I seem a little sharper. The doctor comes in to check on me.

"We've reduced your pain medication. Your scans are fine, so your mother is coming to take you home. Your hand will mend just fine, but you'll be in the cast for several weeks," the doctor says.

They put me in a wheelchair, as my mom and the nurse wheel me out of the hospital and to the car.

On the way out, I look around the hallway, but everything still seems hazy, like I'm seeing through smudged glasses. I think I see Amanda's parents as I go by, but truthfully, they're the only ones I would recognize, since I met them before.

"Are those Amanda's parents, Mom? Is she going home too?" I ask.

"Those are her parents, but no, I think she's staying in the hospital a little longer," she says.

On the drive back home, I stare at the road ahead. I start to remember little bits and pieces and feel a tear stream down my face.

A few days later, my head is clearer and Taylor brings me a vase full of roses and a bag of my favorite candy.

"Remember that candy store we went to with…" he says and stops himself. We went with Ashley and Ryan.

It's sweet and I'm flattered he remembered.

We watch a movie together, but I tire easily, so he leaves. It's nice to see his smiling face. This is the first normalcy I've had since the accident.

I miss his texts—they make me laugh. My phone was destroyed in the accident, so life feels very quiet. My mom ordered me a new one and it should be here any day. I miss the connection, but the silence is peaceful.

Sitting alone gives me time to focus my mind. I keep getting little clips of memory, but nothing for sure. It's like a puzzle I may not want to finish.

But I finally grasp what happened to Ashley. I cry for a long while. I don't understand it. It all seems so pointless and yet so final. People my age don't die.

I still don't remember the accident, and maybe I never will, but the reality of the consequences is penetrating my thoughts.

"Melinda, Ashley's parents phoned with the details of her funeral. Do you feel up to it?" my mom asks.

"I'm going," I say calmly and definitively. I don't need to think about it. No matter how I feel, I have to be there.

I've never been to a funeral before. My family isn't particularly religious, but maybe I was too young before. I still think I'm too young now. I don't know what to expect.

Ashley's parents asked everyone to wear pink in her memory. It is—was—her favorite color. She always said it looked great with her coloring, and since it's the color of bubble gum, it's fun and made her feel good inside.

As I look through my clothes, I pick out a pink dress I got on one of our shopping excursions. I hope it makes me feel good inside, but today, that's not likely.

Popularity

When we drive up to the funeral place, there are cars as far as the eye can see and a line of people around the building in a sea of pink. At first, I smile seeing everyone dressed in her color. She'd like that.

But I'm confused by the line. I recognize some kids from school and the girls from poms. Is everyone here to pay tribute to her? Do kids my age normally go to funerals?

As one of the pallbearers, her brother ushers my mom and me into the building. The place is mobbed with adults and kids—family, friends of her parents and tons and tons of kids from school.

I'm astounded. Her brother shows us to a smaller line for close friends and family.

Standing there, I don't know what to think. It's all so bizarre. I don't know if it's my medication or me, but it all seems to be playing out like some kind of surreal play. It doesn't seem real.

I look around at her parents and grandparents standing there looking stoic, greeting everyone like an assembly line.

It's the strangest custom. The grieving family has to put on a dog and pony show and shake every hand to accept their condolences. I don't know if I could do that.

As we get closer to the front, I get nervous. I don't know what to say. "Sorry" just doesn't seem enough. Should I say how much I like her or what a great friend she is—was—is? But I don't want them to feel bad. I don't want to make this experience worse for them.

The butterflies in my stomach seem like jet planes flying back and forth as I get to the front of the line, and then I feel a hand grasp mine. I turn—it's Ev.

"I thought you may need a friend," she says.

I do need a friend. And she has pink in her hair. Since I don't think she has any pink clothes, I appreciate the sentiment.

We shake Ashley's parents' and grandparents' hands and I look at her mother. Her face is sullen and pale. I can see she's been crying, but she's doing her best to stay strong and get through the day.

"She's a really good friend to me," I say as I take her hand.

She thanks me. I really feel terrible for all of them—to have to grieve so publicly. I just don't get it.

Now it's time to say goodbye to Ashley. I stop and hesitate a little, but my mom and Ev squeeze my hands and give me strength.

Popularity

There's Ashley lying there looking peaceful and angelic, like she's just sleeping. She's wearing the pink sequin dress she made for the last dance. Her poms uniform and her poms are beside her along with her partially made wedding dress.

I think she'd like that. But looking at the future she'll never have make it clear. She's never going to get married, graduate, go to prom or college, or have kids. She'll never do anything she thought she would. It's so final.

"Wow, she looks perfect. There's not a scratch on her," Ev whispers to me in surprise.

As soon as she says it, she immediately looks at me, realizing her slip of the tongue. But only I hear her and she's right. She looks beautiful, untouched while the rest of us are bruised, banged and bandaged, but alive.

I remember something I overheard in the hallway earlier. A man say she hit her head and was dead on impact. None of it makes sense, but it's a little comfort to think she didn't feel anything.

I get a little dizzy and start to sway a bit. My mom and Ev get me to a nearby chair out in the lobby. Ev hands me some water.

Then I hear two men talking nearby.

"At the speed they were going, if it was only 10 seconds later, they would have been clear."

All sudden, everything rushes back to me. The whole accident plays right before my eyes like a movie. The truck smashed into the side Ashley was on. It was a direct hit to her door. I remember everything and gasp for breath. Tears slowly fall from the corners of my eyes and stream down my face.

We sit for a while and watch the crowd. The room is filled with beautiful pink and white flower arrangements and wreaths everywhere. Someone says every poms team from nearby schools sent flowers. That's really nice.

A little girl comes up to us and asks if we want to buy a pink bracelet as part of a fundraiser for the funeral costs. It says "Dance Forever, Ashley" with the date she died. My mom takes one for me and gives the girl some money. Ev buys one too, puts it on her wrist. She never knew Ashley or understood my friendship with her, but I really appreciate her support.

Sitting there, we watch the huge line of people continue to infinity.

"I guess that's one of the perks of being popular—you get a big crowd at your funeral," Ev says in a soft, somber voice.

Ev is very honest and has a tendency to openly say what many people think. It get's her into trouble sometimes, but she's right.

It's so strange. Ashley is popular as a member of The Glam Squad and the poms team. But she didn't know all these people and they didn't know her. I guess they knew *of* her.

I can't figure it out. I see some people go back in line after they went through and notice the kids talking in line. Then I realize—it's like an event. See and be seen.

Soon, Ashley's brother takes me to a different room with the other pallbearers so we can get instructions. My mom and Ev will wait for me. With my arm, I won't lift anything—it's mostly symbolic.

As soon as I walk in, I see Ryan and Taylor. Ryan looks like a zombie. He's sitting there staring straight ahead and Taylor has his arm around him, comforting him.

Ryan's whole life has changed too. His plans with Ashley are gone. Thinking about it makes me shake my head with sadness.

It's all so needless, so unnecessary. I just don't understand why. Why the accident? Why her? She was just sitting there. She wasn't driving. And it wasn't her fault.

I see the other glam girls in the room. Chloe's on crutches with a broken ankle. Brittany's in a wheelchair with her leg and arm in casts. I feel awful, as the impact of my falling on top of her against the car door probably worsened her injuries. But just like everyone else, I'm an innocent victim too.

The only one who isn't innocent is Amanda. She's sitting on the other side of the room straight up stiff in a chair; her broken ribs must be heavily wrapped under her clothes. Her hair is pulled to one side, trying to cover her bandaged face, black eye and broken nose.

Alyssa is there too. I bet she's glad she went ahead to the game and wasn't in the car crash. Or maybe she feels guilty. I don't know.

Sometimes I wonder why no one else died. I was right next to Ashley. Amanda was on the same side as her. My mom says no one's to blame and I shouldn't feel guilty, but I'm not sure. I keep hearing the man's words pound in my head—just 10 seconds and we would've been fine.

Popularity

While we're waiting, Alyssa tells me Amanda has to wait another few weeks to have plastic surgery to fix her face. She has a big scar on the side of her cheek from the windshield.

I stare at her a little. I can't help wondering what Amanda's thinking. I'm sure she's sad about Ashley too, but does she feel responsible? Is she sorry?

As the day goes on, my anger at Amanda builds, but I don't say anything. Every time I see her, I want to know if she regrets texting while driving. There were so many ifs. If she hadn't looked at her phone. If she'd paid more attention, she would've seen the stop sign. If she'd not been so worried about being late for the poms performance… What-ifs are useless. It happened, but did it have to? If the truck had been there 10 seconds later, it would have missed the car. Ten lousy seconds.

I look out the room and I see Rachel standing there and walk out to see her.

"I heard you broke your arm. Does it hurt?" she says, pointing to my cast.

"No, it'll be fine. I'll be ok," I say and we stand there for a moment in awkward silence.

"I'm glad you came," I say.

"I don't really want to see anyone, but I felt I had to come. I'm trying to stay out of the way. I really don't know how to pay my respects and stay out of the way from the crowd," she says.

I take her hand and squeeze it and look her in the eyes.

"Rachel. You have no reason to hide. You did nothing. You were wronged. Take it from someone who has been bullied. You need to show them they can't break you," I say.

She drops her head with uncertainty, so I tell her about how Caroline and her other friends stood up for her. And I fill her in on what the football players did to Ev at the game and to her house.

"She's not going to let them win. If you change your life because of them, only you lose," I say and she glances up to me.

"I saw Caroline in line. Maybe we can catch up to her," I say and she nods. I brought her out to the line and left her with Caroline before I went back to the room. I think she'll be ok. It's a first step.

Popularity

The next week I go back to school. My cast will still be on my wrist and hand for a few more weeks, but luckily, since I'm a lefty, I can still write. It's tough to get shirts and jackets on and off, but I'm getting used to it.

My mom insists on driving me to school to make sure I get there ok. She brings Ev too, since she takes me to class and holds my books. They've both been very attentive and protective of me since the crash, waiting on me and helping me with everything.

When we pull up, I see it for the first time. There on the front lawn of the school is Amanda's crunched car—what's left of it.

I gaze at it with curious wonder. The back of the driver's side where the truck hit is pushed in like someone punched it. There's no glass anywhere in the car. My mom tells me whatever glass wasn't shattered in the crash was broken by emergency services to pull the rest of us out. I think I must have been unconscious then.

It's weird. What once was a sparkly and expensive SUV is now garbage, like the junk that's piled on a heap in the scrapyard.

My mom says the size of the car probably saved the rest of us. So, is it savior or tomb? Or both?

As I stand there in frozen silence, Ev puts her arm around me.

"Let's go in now; you don't have to see this. I can't believe the school thought it was a good idea to put it here. It's cruel," she says and pulls on my good hand.

"No, I need a minute," I say and keep staring.

I notice that there's a sign in front of the wreckage. It says "In memory of Ashley Carroll. Remember, don't text and drive. It can wait."

We enter the school, but the entire day, I can't get that line out of my head. *It can wait.*

It rings in my ear and resonates in my head. Just like the what-ifs I contemplated at the funeral. If Amanda waited, if she wasn't so worried about letting them know we were coming, it wouldn't have happened. Ashley would be alive. If only.

Seeing the car again so soon is a little unnerving, but I can see what the school's thinking. If it prevents one kid from making the same mistake, it's worth it. Because it was just a stupid mistake.

I dread lunchtime, as I'll see everyone again. I'm going to sit with Ev and her friends, but I want to say hi to the glam girls, just to see how they're doing.

Popularity

I sit for a minute and talk to Alyssa, Chloe and Brittany. Then Amanda comes over in a huff.

"I'm tired of being a freak show!" she yells and slams her bag on the table. "They're staring at me all the time. I can't wait to get my surgery and get my life and looks back. Then they'll see."

In an instant, I feel all the rage from the last week gurgle up inside me like a volcano ready to erupt. I would've thought maybe the tragedy taught her a lesson, but now I know it didn't.

I start to breathe heavily and seethe, her false victimization and selfish vanity echoing in my head until I explode.

"This is not all about you! Ashley will never get her life back. Her family and Ryan will never be the same and it's all your fault! You killed her. Your popularity killed her. Your whole life revolves around how and what people think of you. Maintaining that high pedestal is too hard to keep from falling off. I fell for it all hook, line and sinker but now I see it's shallow. Being a part of The Glam Squad and being popular is the highlight of your life. Not for me. For Ashley, it's all been taken away because of one senseless mistake.

It's just too high a price to pay. Friendships, family, life are way more important than any of this. I pity you."

After the last words come out of my mouth, I walk to Ev's and sit down with my head on the table.

I'm gutted. I can't even breathe and barely remember what I said. It just came out.

"It needed to be said," Ev says and pats my head with approval. "Welcome back."

Popularity

Chapter Fifteen
New Day

As I review the past eight months, it seems like a roller coaster of great highs, scary bumps, thrilling loops and plummeting lows. Or maybe it's more like a merry-go-round. I'm spinning around, sitting on a beautiful pony, waving at the crowd as they admire me and the popular girls. We twirl around and around, but we're always staying in the same place. That's not enough for me. I want to move and grow.

Somehow, I feel like myself again. And for the first time in a while, I want to draw. Everything in my head and my heart has to come out in my art.

I sit at my desk in my bedroom and roll out some paper, keeping it attached to the spool on my desk. The entire weekend I focus intently, with my pencils furiously wearing down to nubs as I keep pulling more and more paper. I'm obsessed. I don't look at my new phone and barely take breaks. My mom brings me food, I think. There's no plan, I just keep sketching. I have to get it all out. Everything.

By Sunday night, I take a deep breath and rest my head back on my chair. I look at the curling waves of piled paper on the ground. I pull them all out and stretch the paper across the room to see what I did. I look at it as if I'm seeing it for the first time, but it all makes sense.

It shows beautiful people laughing and swinging around a carousel with their hair gently flowing in the breeze. They wave to the people who are surrounding them in admiration, waving back.

Then there's a roller coaster going up and down. At the top, the beautiful people are happy and carefree, but as they go down, their hair stands straight up and their eyes bulge in terror. At the bottom, it's over. And there's nothing. A dark empty desolate gray park with small sprouting pink flowers.

My mom comes in and looks over my shoulder.

"Wow, that's really something. I think it's your best work ever." She pauses and gazes at it. "What do you call it?"

"Popularity," I say.

My ride is complete.

Now Ev and I are back in the groove. And Taylor and I talk and go to the movies, but not on Friday nights. That's my time with Ev and I'll never neglect that again. We're best friends forever. Maybe I'll invite Ev to come with us sometime. Like a double date.

At lunch the following week, Alyssa unexpectedly comes up to me, surprising everyone at Ev's lunch table into hushed silence.

"I hope you don't mind the interruption, but we've been working on an idea," she says. "Rachel is back at poms now and we talked about the accident and got this brainstorm. Turns out Rachel's family owns a beauty products company that sells nail polish and the company is going to give a huge discount on bottles of nail polish. We're going to do a big promotion to increase awareness for texting and driving and raise money for school supplies for kids who can't afford them. It's called The Thumbs UP Ashley Project."

A warm pleasant sense washes over me.

"How can I help?" I ask.

"We need a logo for the bottles and thought you can draw something," she says.

Immediately I know what I want to do. I take out my sketchbook and quickly scribble a blossoming pink rose with swirling lines incorporating Ashley's name.

"How about something like this? I'll make it look better; this is just an idea" I say and show her the drawing.

"That's perfect," she says as she hugs me.

"The campaign is called Thumbs UP—Don't Text and Drive. We're encouraging girls to paint their thumbnails a different color to remind them not to text while driving," she explains.

"Just girls?" Ev asks in disagreement.

Alyssa looks at her with a warm smile.

"Everyone," she says.

"I think that's a great idea. Count me in," Ev says with excitement.

In a couple weeks, we set up a couple tables at lunchtime. There are three shades of sparkly pink nail polish called The Ashley line. The logo I drew of a blossoming rose with stars around it is on every bottle with Ashley's name. That's how I see her. A beautiful flower that will keep blooming forever in my mind.

From that beginning, the word spreads like wildfire. Rachel expands the effort by recruiting poms teams from different schools all over the state to set up tables. I'm glad to see her back at school and as the poms captain. And no one said anything to her. The dean's crackdown and new policies have curbed the bulling and cyberbulling.

But the big push comes from the most unlikely source—Amanda. She has been out of school for a month, getting plastic surgery on her face. We haven't spoken since my blowup. But Alyssa says she wants to help, so even with the bandages over her face, Amanda records videos of the mangled car, shows pictures of Ashley and tells our story, admitting her mistake. She promotes The Thumbs UP Ashley Project to her thousands and thousands of followers, who share it with others.

I never thought she'd show her face on camera while it's healing. It's an amazing transformation of character.

The Thumbs UP Ashley Project is going well. The nail polish manufacturer launched a website for us and linked it to all their advertising and we've received a ton of recognition from the town and the media. But the big difference came when Amanda got a social media celebrity on board.

A huge fashion influencer stitched one of Amanda's TikTok videos and sent it out to her millions of viewers, encouraging the project. Then she DM'd Amanda asking how she could help further.

From there, it takes off like a rocket. The influencer posts more videos promoting The Thumbs UP Ashley Project and even adds a petition to have everyone sign pledging not to text and drive. It's working.

By the end of the school year, The Thumbs UP Ashley Project sells one million bottles of nail polish. The website features several celebrity endorsements and a running total of all the kids who pledged not to text and drive.

And Chloe tells me we raised enough money to pay for school supplies for many poor schools in the state. I think Ashley would like that.

"In a way, it honors her. We always felt bad that she didn't have as much money as we do and wanted to pay tribute to that struggle," Brittany says.

Popularity

I drop my jaw in shock.

"You knew about her?"

"Yes, we all knew. We never said anything because we didn't want her to feel awkward. She was one of us, no matter what," she says and nods her head, smiling.

I can't believe it. Maybe I misjudged their shallowness and elitist emphasis on money. They accepted Ashley for herself, in spite of her means. After all, they did the same for me, knowing my situation.

It's been quite a year. Amanda, Chloe and Alyssa graduated. At the ceremony, they left a place for Ashley with her picture, and her mom accepted her diploma. The choir sang an old song to her, "Forever Young."

I decide not to go to any of their graduation parties—I don't want to get sucked into their rich world again. It's too easy to get lost. But I want to count them as friends, so I send them all drawings of them in their caps and gowns.

A week later, the yearbook comes out with my drawings on the poms pages and a special section dedicated to Ashley with her senior picture surrounded by a special drawing I made for her. Ev made up a poem and they put it on the last page.

In the sunshine and flowers you will always be there;
Smiling and laughing like you have no cares;
Peaceful and joyous your soul will be;
Our guardian angel in the sky we'll see...

I frame a copy the picture and the poem and send it to her parents with an illustration of her beautiful face coming out of pink roses and other flowers on hilly green paths with sunshine beaming everywhere, reflecting in pools of shimmering blue water.

Her grandfather told me at her funeral that she was always a ray of sunshine that sparkled into their lives every day. I'd like to believe she's in a place like that.

As I thumb through the yearbook, it's like reliving the year. I started a wallflower, became a glam girl, and ended as something else. I'm not sure what yet, but I know I'm wiser.

The one thing that stays in my mind is... was it worth it?

I craved popularity from afar and envied them all so much, but when it I got it, it wasn't what I expected.

Thinking about it makes my head hurt. Why did it matter to me so much?

Popularity

It turned out the girls aren't as empty and shallow as Ev thought and their friendship for me and each other is real, but somehow it still doesn't seem to matter. Popularity is a façade. It isn't real.

Ev knew about that right from the beginning. It doesn't matter what other people think of me. Only I can be my biggest fan—the hero of my own story. I don't need adulation from others.

And if I ever forget, I'll just look down at Ashley's pink bracelet on my wrist to remind me to be myself.

For the summer, I go back to my job babysitting and working a few hours at the boxing plant. But I'm also having some fun with Taylor, Ev and seeing the glam girls sometimes. I don't want to be engulfed in their world anymore, but I want to stay friends with them and the poms girls.

When I get home from babysitting at the end of June, my mom's waiting for me with a big smile on her face and a letter in her hand.

"Here—it came!" she says, practically jumping up and down with glee.

Confused, but happily curious, I take the letter. It says…

"Congratulations, you have been accepted into the Keane College of Arts with a full scholarship."

I look at my mom, speechless with a goofy smile on my face, and hug her. We both scream and jump up and down with excitement.

When we stop, I pull back and shake my head to see if it's real.

"How did this happen? I missed the deadline. I didn't submit anything," I say.

"I did. When I saw the wonderful deep and honest illustration you drew after the accident, I emailed the dean of students, explained what happened, and submitted a copy of the drawing," she explains with ecstatic pride.

The letter says they want to see more of my work and recommend an online incubation program where I can get feedback from their professors and participate in some mentoring programs and exhibitions. And after I graduate from high school, a scholarship will be waiting.

I can't believe it.

I think I've grown 10 years over the last 12 months and learned enough for a whole adolescence.

Popularity

I spent my first year of high school dreaming of being popular and my sophomore year being popular. I think for my junior year, I'll just be me. It's a new day.

Check out more of the Growing UP Girls Series.

Book 1: Diary of a 6th Grade "C" Cup—Growing up gets a lot tougher when she's the first in class to get a bra.

Book 2: The One and Only Skizitz—She marches to her own drummer and doesn't care what other people think.

https://www.amazon.com/gp/product/B08N5WZ7JG?ref_=dbs_p_mng_rwt_ser_shvlr&storeType=ebooks

What's Next?

The Growing UP Girls Series has many more stories to tell about girls of all ages. Here are the books coming up. I'd be interested to know from my readers—what do you want to see next from these? I'm always welcome to ideas for other books.

Nerdy Norah—Norah is really smart. She loves math and science and enjoys getting gold stars from teachers and being on the top honor roll lists. But as she gets older, she finds the disadvantages of being smart—especially that some boys don't like smart girls.

It's All a Game?—Gina loves gaming. She always pursues it with friends and alone. When she gets to high school and joins the Egames club, she's thrilled to be among her people. She levels up and up and experiences the good, the bad and the ugly of the gaming world.

Chatty Cassie—Cassie is a people person. She likes to talk and loves to gossip. She ignores teachers hassling her about talking in class and branches out to online forums,

Popularity

but when her chatty ways turn on her, she finds the being the source of the information can be wonderful and horrible at the same time.

Reflection

Ten years ago, my beautiful sweet 16-year-old niece died in a car accident. She was texting while driving alone and was hit in the driver's side door by a truck when she failed to see the stoplight turn red as she approached an intersection.

This is not her story, but I always blamed her popularity for what happened; that she felt so compelled to stay connected online at all times that she couldn't disconnect even for a few moments. But I eventually realized, it was just a mistake, although a costly one.

It's taken me a decade to summon the courage to write about her accident and many tears were shed on my keyboard in the process.

But as I write these stories about girls growing up, I wanted to include some perilous truths about consequences of actions and offer something to consider.

Popularity has its benefits and can give a wonderful experience, but as Shakespeare says, "To thine own self be true."

Popularity

If you give up who you are and sacrifice yourself for a chance in the limelight—or if you needlessly hurt others just because they aren't like you—it's a high price to pay for all. And sometimes it's too much.

It's easy to get wrapped up in the rewards of being part of a group and the social media frenzy of teenage existence but keep your eye on the ball at all times. And put yourself in other people's shoes. Variety is the best part of life. Thumbs UP.

Why Bully?

"If you read up on the causes of bullying there are many articles which discuss the lack of ability to recognize distress in others and the problems with anger and behavioral disruption kids experience that lead to bullying behaviors. What I believe happens on a more frequent basis and what I see happening in the lives of my clients, my child, and what I experienced as a kid are the microaggressions that build up and cause harm. It is the whispered comments, the looks given, and the nicknames given that the building hurt and harm is found. The statement often put out there is kids are mean. The question less asked is where does that meanness come from? Sometimes it comes from the environment; the child sees it or hears it and they mimic it, not understanding the full gravity of their doing. Other times it is a fear or weakness that drives it. What I can say definitively affects it is how this is addressed by parents, primary schools, and everyone as you get older. If kids are taught to be kind, to be aware of differences in a way that evokes compassion, not judgment or weirdness, these things would happen less. The struggle is when parents do not know how to do this, how would we teach the children? Start with the recognition that everyone is different. Lead with the introduction that this is beautiful, not wrong."

Sarah Decker,
Licensed Marriage and Family Therapist

About the Author

Thank you for reading this book. I like to tell stories about different girls growing up. It's not easy. There are perils and pitfalls everywhere, but there are also successes. The best thing you can do is to always #beyourself.

I encourage everyone to make their own path in life, no matter what age. I did, but it took a long time.

I spent my first career trying to find my bliss in journalism, public relations, real estate, and marketing. Now I'm enjoying my second career—writing. I write in many genres for all ages, but I always try to tell stories of everyday life experiences in a fun-filled read. Originally from Chicago, my husband and I, along with my computer, are happy transplants in the warm and gentle breezes of Southwest Florida.

Please let me know what you think with a review on Bookbub.com or Goodreads.com or Amazon.com at https://www.amazon.com/review/create-review?&asin=B0B3SJ8NGH. I value the opinions of my readers and will always strive to entertain and give you a good feeling after the last page is read.

Feel free to reach out to me on my social media channels and sign up for my newsletter to get weekly short stories, bonus materials, name and book cover reveals and contests, giveaways, and exclusive sneak peeks and updates on new releases. I love to hear from my readers. You can sign up and find out what I'm working on and get some behind the pages information at *www.suzanneruddhamilton.com*. You can also follow me on social media at:

@suzanneruddhamilton

@suzanneruddhamilton

@suzruddhamilton

Suzanne Rudd Hamilton, Author

@suzanneruddhamilton

@suzanneruddhamilton

My Other Works

Welcome to my world. I write stories for young adult and middle grade girls under the name Suzanne Rudd.

Middle-Grade/Young Adult: Suzanne Rudd

The Growing UP Girls Series:

Book 1: Diary of a 6th Grade "C" Cup
Book 2: The One and Only Skizitz
Book 3: Popularity

Children's Picture Books: Suzanne Rudd

How an Angel Gets Its Wings

I also write cozy mysteries, women's fiction, historical romances, books for middle grades and young adults and children's illustrated books as Suzanne Rudd Hamilton. My books are clean and friendly for any audience. If you want to read more from me, here are my works. All novels are available in paperback and eBook on Amazon.com and Kindle and soon to be available as audiobooks through Amazon.com/Audible and ITunes:

Romance: Suzanne Rudd Hamilton

A Timeless American Historical Romance Series:

Book 1: The Sailor and the Songbird
Book 2: Irish Eyes

Book 3: The Summer of Love (June 2023 release)

First Sight: Contemporary Stories of Love

Women's Fiction: Suzanne Rudd Hamilton

The Little Shoppes Books Series:

Book 1: Cupcakes, etc.
Book 2: Butterfly Bridal Boutique (Jan 2023 release)

Cozy/Detective Mystery: Suzanne Rudd Hamilton

Secret Senior Sleuths Society Series:

Book 1: Puzzle at Peacock Perch
Book 2: Peril at Peacock Perch (2022 release)

Beck's Rules Mysteries Series:

Book 1: Beck's Rules

I also write plays for the performing arts: *Hollywood Whodunnit*; *Death, Debauchery and Dinner*; *Dames are Dangerous*; *Puzzle at Peacock Perch; Sounds and Silence;* and the musical *Welcome Home*.

With Love and Appreciation

This book is dedicated to my family and friends who help me break down obstacles, jump over hurdles, and leap ahead—and who pick me up each time I get knocked down.

Thanks to my "Pens" and other writer friends and colleagues for your encouragement and direction.

And to my safety nets, editor Andie and cover artist Elizabeth, and all my ARC and beta readers—thanks for all your invaluable input and support.

To my readers, thanks for coming along on the ride.

Printed in Great Britain
by Amazon